Thinking Ahead

Other Books by These Authors

Thinking Beyond the Test: Strategies for Re-Introducing Higher-Level Thinking Skills

Focus on Thinking: Engaging Students in Higher-Order Thinking

Thinking Ahead

Engaging All Teachers in Critical Thinking

Paul A. Wagner, Daphne Johnson, Frank Fair, and Daniel Fasko Jr.

ROWMAN & LITTLEFIELD
Lanham • Boulder • New York • London

Published by Rowman & Littlefield
A wholly owned subsidiary of The Rowman & Littlefield Publishing Group, Inc.
4501 Forbes Boulevard, Suite 200, Lanham, Maryland 20706
www.rowman.com

Unit A, Whitacre Mews, 26–34 Stannary Street, London SE11 4AB

Copyright © 2018 by Paul A. Wagner, Daphne Johnson, Frank Fair and Daniel Fasko Jr.

All rights reserved. No part of this book may be reproduced in any form or by any electronic or mechanical means, including information storage and retrieval systems, without written permission from the publisher, except by a reviewer who may quote passages in a review.

British Library Cataloguing in Publication Information Available

Library of Congress Cataloging-in-Publication Data
Names: Wagner, Paul A., 1947–
Title: Thinking ahead : engaging all teachers in critical thinking /
  Paul A. Wagner, Daphne Johnson, Frank Fair, and Daniel Fasko Jr.
Description: Lanham : Rowman & Littlefield, [2018] |
  Includes bibliographical references and index.
Identifiers: LCCN 2018000470 (print) | LCCN 2018001048 (ebook) |
  ISBN 9781475841022 (electronic) | ISBN 9781475841008 (cloth : alk. paper) |
  ISBN 9781475841015 (pbk. : alk. paper)
Subjects: LCSH: Critical thinking—Study and teaching. | Teachers—Training of.
Classification: LCC LB1590.3 (ebook) | LCC LB1590.3 .W338 2018 (print) |
  DDC 372.47/4—dc23
LC record available at https://lccn.loc.gov/2018000470

∞™ The paper used in this publication meets the minimum requirements of American National Standard for Information Sciences—Permanence of Paper for Printed Library Materials, ANSI/NISO Z39.48–1992.

Printed in the United States of America

Paul A. Wagner would like to dedicate this book to his son, Jason, who has been a natural teacher all of his life. Also to Phoenix, his stepdaughter, who keeps life exciting, and to Joshua, his stepson, who keeps all calm in the midst of turbulence and to my grandchildren Colin, Caiden and Alyssa Wallace.

Daphne Johnson would like to dedicate this book to her children, Tucker and M. J. Watching you both grow and develop cognitively, emotionally, and physically has been amazing. Thank you both for all the learning experiences.

Frank Fair would like to dedicate this book to his grandchildren, Nathan, Emma, and Emily. They are three bright rays of hope for the future.

Daniel Fasko Jr. dedicates this book to his daughters, Heather Fasko-McMillan and Kathryn Fasko, who have made me "think" about possibilities. They have also given me plenty of opportunities to make decisions, some that were not as productive as we would have liked them to be and others that were positive and benefited them in their growth and me in my growth as a parent. He also dedicates this book to his grandsons, Malcolm Daniel McMillan and David Lee McMillan.

Contents

Acknowledgments		ix
Introduction		xi
1	What Is a Good Education?	1
2	Current Realities	17
3	Values and Critical Thinking	29
4	Education at the Crossroads	45
5	Critico-Creative Thinking: Tools and Strategies	55
6	Preservice Teacher Preparation Scripts	75
Appendix A: Resources for Further Information: An Annotated List		117
Appendix B: What You Wanted to Know about Action Research but Were Afraid to Ask		123
Appendix C: A Note to Professors on Building Their Own Scripts		125
References		135
Index		147

Acknowledgments

The success of this team is due in part to the patience and persistence of individuals involved. Other success is due to technology. Some of us met one another nearly thirty years ago or so, and others have never met face-to-face. Nonetheless each acquired experience with the topic, the scripts, and the research literature and edited one another's work until this volume came to speak with one voice.

Paul Wagner wants first to acknowledge Lawrence Kohlberg. Through working with Larry at every level of his projects and even team teaching with him for a short time at Harvard, Wagner learned much about effective teacher education and involving teachers with on-site experience under the watchful eye of a mentor. Kohlberg and Matt Lipman often saw one another as rivals. I was pleased to arrange for Matt to give a talk at Larry's Center for Moral Development, and the three of us had dinner afterward. While I kept in touch with each, that was the only time the two ever met. The contrast between the two became an important part of my education and a source of insight for this book. Lipman had a worthy and ambitious vision for education, while Kohlberg had a greater sense of teacher training and making a shared vision happen among his trainees.

Daphne Johnson sincerely appreciates the patience of the coauthors of the book. Their understanding was priceless to the process. She would also like to thank her wife, Ashley, for her continued support and patience during the writing process.

Frank Fair would like to acknowledge the help and encouragement of numerous philosophy and psychology colleagues over the forty-six years he was privileged to teach in the Department of Psychology and Philosophy at Sam Houston State University. His colleagues' concern for truly educating students, their passion for following the research and the arguments wherever they lead, and their doing all of this with grace and good humor made the department a truly remarkable environment in which to teach and to learn. Frank would also like to acknowledge his son-in-law, Anthony Lupinetti, for providing much-needed technical assistance at just the right time.

Daniel Fasko is grateful for the opportunity to collaborate on this and other books with my coauthors. He is eternally grateful to his wife, Sharla, for her editorial assistance and endless patience and support with him and his writing endeavors. She is truly a saint!

We would also like to thank Thomas Koerner and Carlie Wall of Rowman and Littlefield publishers for their encouragement, thoughtful comments, and assistance with this book.

Introduction

By the second decade of the twenty-first century, Phillip Jackson (2011) wrote a widely circulated book titled *What Is Education?* One cannot help but wonder why there was such a response to this book leading to its being reissued in paperback in 2016. Is it not obvious to everyone what education is?

On the surface, this would seem to be a question already answered in simple and compact fashion. Western nations are spending billions of dollars on high-stakes standardized tests for students at every age. If classical economic theory is right and how we spend our money is the meta-language of what we value, then Jackson's question is answered by noting success on these massive examinations. And, after all, what would be wrong about such a conclusion?

If students never learned any facts or principles in the classroom, that would surely suggest education had failed. But there is reason to think there is more to education than success on recognition tests. There must be broad application of what is learned, and there is yet more. There must be a continued passion to review critically all that has been learned, and there must be passion to continue learning more. Without these latter elements, education is a failure. Success in these latter elements starts with teacher training (Perkins, Jay, & Tishman, 1993).

This book addresses a very important aspect of teacher training, as well as the training of educational administrators, school counselors, and other educationally allied professionals, which is too often overlooked. That aspect is role-modeling a deliberative mind. A deliberative mind is one filled with wonderment and eagerness to learn. We introduce educational professionals to systematic, pondering, and large-scale wonderment.

It is tempting to do as Jackson did and cite sources of antiquity taking the reader through a grand tour of history to some magnificent claims about the purpose and meaning of education. Our mission is different and more modest.

We introduce educational professionals to deliberative reasoning. The upshot of this effort is twofold. First, we show teachers how to become more deliberative about their consumption of pedagogical advice and sense of purpose. Second, we show teachers how to take advantage of teachable moments and role-model critico-creative thinking.

The scripted discussions in chapter 6 systematically engage readers in opportunities to learn from one another's deep thinking. These engagements show that even when discussion cannot settle on grand truths, discussion that leads away from errant ideas is invaluable.

Historically there are two figures in intellectual history who are not typically associated with teacher-training but who are essentially relevant to the aspects addressed herein. The first person is a sixteenth-century scientist, Blaise Pascal. Pascal is referenced in most books on decision theory and cognitive science and business management books as the father of decision making under conditions of uncertainty (e.g., Hacking, 2006). The second person is a nineteenth-century logician, Charles Dodgson, better known to most as Lewis Carroll, the author of *Alice in Wonderland*, the poem "Jabberwocky," and other classics of English literature. Dodgson was all about adventures in conceptual wonderment.

Lives are lived in a world that is filled with uncertainty. Nonetheless, a world of uncertainty does not destine each person to live a life randomly determined by fate, karma, or accident. For sure, there will be plenty of unforeseen game changers in the life of each person. However, learning to think systematically can narrow the unintended destructive effects of random chance. Life is full of placing bets. Pascal draws out attention to optimizing chances at placing better bets.

Dodgson is a logician. As such, he appreciates systematic thinking. But Dodgson is mentioned in the context of this book because of how much he favored prompts to speculation and critical review.

As much as today's teachers need to know technology and prepare students for standardized tests, they also need to know how to exploit the experience of wonderment and collaborative review to advance shared understanding with others. Educators need to show students how to eliminate errors in reasoning. Students need to learn ways for optimizing the effectiveness of decisions. These elements of teacher training too often fall through the cracks (Willingham, 2007). We address these needs for educator and student through text and scripted dialogues.

Regardless of advances in the science of thinking strategies, in the end, every thinking strategy must be appraised by standards of critical thinking. For this book, we rely initially on the definition recently proposed by William Gormley in his book from Harvard Educational Press titled *The Critical Advantage*. Gormley (2017) writes:

Critical thinking (or reflective thinking) is an intense mental activity, not a causal one. It requires alertness, patience, and a commitment to accuracy and precision . . . [it] focuses on a belief or set of beliefs or something thought to be true. In effect, we reappraise something that we believe or that others believe. We probe for weaknesses or lapses of logic, flimsy claims. The aim is to subject a subject to a withering stress test, to see whether it can survive a tough cross examination. (p. 15)

And as Gormley further explains, "Critical thinking is not all encompassing, nor is it the only form of higher order thinking" (p. 29). Other forms of higher-order thinking are identified in this book. Because this book concentrates on practice in reflective thinking as it applies to professional pedagogy, we extend the term "higher-order thinking" to include creative thinking.

Creative thinking is artful, hypothetical, and driven by wonderment. The term we use to scaffold all higher-order thinking is "critico-creative thinking." Critico-creative thinking, broadly conceived, is the engine of creation and ultimate review. It constitutes the process of the Great Conversation of Humankind. While the reader will learn some technicalities from the cutting edge of higher-level thinking, the focus of the text always returns to critico-creative thinking as a general strategy for review and planning. Reflective teaching exploits opportunities for role-modeling reflective learning.

The Great Conversation of Humankind is about big questions. Big questions require openness to a broad range of thinking strategies. From antiquity, commitment to what computational scientists at the University of Toronto now call "deep thinking," thinking about thinking and strategies to think better continue to evolve. We now know more about effective thinking and avoiding bad decisions than we ever did in past generations (Almossawi, 2017). Whether through logic, Cartesian geometry, probabilistic analysis to mathematical game theory, or prudent use of heuristical shortcuts, we have in many ways become better at thinking.

Critico-creative thinking is the engine of creation and ultimately of review for all process and product emanating from within the Great Conversation. More proficient skills in critico-creative thinking apply to teaching every subject well. They also open possibilities in the social and moral worlds all people are destined to share with one another.

We could use PowerPoint displays of all the included text and test teachers over the content. But such testing would not prove they learned *how* to do what the text talks about. For this reason, participation in the scripts is key. Teachers cannot take advantage of teachable moments with powerful discussion techniques if they have not participated in them personally. Learning about scripted discussions and teachable moments is a far cry from learning how to manage them.

Text and experience are both important. A British philosopher by the name of Gilbert Ryle offers a nicely fitting analogy. Ryle (1954) invites his readers to remember how they learned to ride a bike. A lecture would not secure the necessary proficiency. Neither would simply watching others ride. Finally, simply getting on a bicycle in a race for experience would most likely lead to injury. To learn to ride a bicycle, you had to have features explained to you. You had to watch others ride a bike successfully. And, eventually you had to give bike-riding a try yourself. So it is with learning to participate in scripted discussions and how to take advantage of teachable moments.

Read on. There is an intellectual adventure ahead for you and then, thanks to you, for your students one day, too.

Chapter 1

What Is a Good Education?

EDUCATION MAY BE ON THE VERGE OF GREAT CHANGE

Education may be on the verge of a change more dramatic than anyone could have anticipated (Cuban, 2016). The change is not the result of political or special interest groups using schooling to drive home contrived agendas. That sort of influence affected education for as long as there has been any institutional history to document such activities (McDonnell & Weatherford, 2016). But this time things are different.

The intensity of the special interest groups and their range may be surging at the moment (Coburn, Hill, & Spillane, 2016), but all this pales in comparison to the forces that are shaping a new image of what it means to be human, forces shaping a new image of what it means to become a better human being through education (Baker, 2011). From psychology to evolutionary theory, what makes a better human is being advocated not just by philosophers and clerics but by renowned scientists as well (Dennett, 2017; Nowak & Highfield, 2011; Peterson & Seligman, 2003).

In addition, algorithmic and technological innovations are changing how humans think of human nature (Domingos, 2015). The much-heralded computer revolution led by consulting educationists and computer corporations is finding the opportunities for further profit grinding down to a near-glacial pace (Hacker, 2016). While consultants and computer delivery systems continue to bring an extraordinary range of knowledge online and in increasingly clever and imaginative formats, measurements of increased student ability are lacking (King, 2016; Smith, 2016). So where is the evidence of intellectual progress amid all this technological razzle-dazzle?

There is only so much that can be done to test for knowledge. Multiple-choice items can test for student ability to identify Newton's laws of motion, or the parts of a eukaryotic cell or the divisions of American government, but such knowledge alone is inert when it comes to understanding challenges of participating in the world.

Nonetheless, despite the need for more dynamic and interactive learning, mere information retrieval remains at the heart of high-stakes, standardized testing and hence educational evaluation (Glass, 2016). This is increasingly making schools look like nineteenth-century schools centering a curriculum around routines of drill and grill, albeit with expensive new wardrobe and accouterments for analogically the same old practices. We will return to this topic in later chapters.

Amazon's Echo and Apple's Siri do their best to deliver accurate facts when solicited for precise information. Blunt statements of fact in the absence of supporting explanation are fast becoming the norm in human knowledge-seeking engagements. The claim to know too often goes unchallenged when delivered by recognized search engines. Contexts of knowledge application are similarly overlooked when blunt statements of fact seem to summarize all that matters.

Deliberative speech is giving way to litanies of declarative utterances. Reflection is giving way to semblances of recognition. Surely there is more schools can do for students than test for their ability to recognize or retrieve information. Surely there are intellectual skills, dispositions, and ambitions that can be taught and that will lead to greater student skill when evaluating information retrieved from a variety of search engines and aggregated in some useable form by individual knowledge-seekers.

IS EDUCATION CHANGING OR SIMPLY BEING REDUCED TO RETRIEVAL PROCESSES?

The problems alluded to above do not exist solely in the nation's public schools. Consider the plight of professional medical education as an example of the extensiveness of the increasing unwitting reliance on algorithm-driven technology. The ubiquitous stethoscope and lab coat for medical residents are now accented with smartphones.

Even in teaching hospitals, Grand Rounds is often dominated by medical students searching their smartphones for answers rather than looking at the patient or the patient's record and then collaboratively deliberating about diagnosis and subsequent prognosis. If standardized observations, blood work, and radiography results can all be scanned into a database for both diagnosis and strategies of prognosis, then why bother with face-to-face patient and doctor engagements?

Indeed, retrieval of information has been greatly aided by the resources of high-powered algorithmic software and computational hardware. Some research has shown that, once a disease context is identified, software diagnosis of patient ailments has proven consistently more accurate than professionally trained human physicians (Christian & Griffiths, 2016). More important, computer algorithms have standards for stopping further searches that optimize decision-making efficiency. This is good thinking at its formalized best. So all is good, right?

Increasingly, people have accepted the idea that computers can think better than humans (Helfland, 2016). And, accordingly, people have accepted the idea that education, inasmuch as it involves the retrieval of relevant information, should focus students' attention on retrieval systems. But there should be more, namely, getting students to think and utilize the retrieved information for some purpose (Syed, 2016).

Educational psychologists nearly a century ago began using the memorization of nonsense syllables to exhibit effectiveness of different learning strategies (Christian & Griffiths, 2016). This led an early cognitivist, George Miller (1956), to study and determine that human computational systems (minds) are typically limited to seven plus or minus two bits of information. When construed as mere retrieval systems, human cognitive capacity explains only memory and limited standard applications. Recent research, however, demonstrates there is much more to cognitive potency (Sapolsky, 2017).

In his book, *Black Box Thinking*, Matthew Syed (2016) explains that "black box thinking" is "about the willingness and tenacity to investigate the lessons that often exist when we fail, but which we rarely exploit. It is about creating systems and cultures that enable organizations to learn from errors, rather than being threatened by them" (p. 31). The optimal potency of thinking requires at the very least that it be self-reflective and open to critical review. The thinking Syed refers to is what we call the Great Conversation of Humankind. In the Great Conversation, cognitive potency, broadly defined, is both process and product of participation. In this Great Conversation, participants exploit the natural urge that humans have to seek patterns that illuminate the unknown (Chomsky & Robichaud, 2014; Christian & Griffiths, 2016).

Such pattern-seeking thinking requires attention to acquired knowledge, as well as insidious flaws that may keep participants' thinking from being more potent. This *flaw-noticing* trait has often been associated with what scholars from C. S. Pierce to Stephen Meyer have termed "abductive thinking" (Meyer, 2013). Abductive thinking neither deduces conclusions as in the case of deductive thinking nor generalizes from examples as in the case of inductive thinking. Abductive thinking is about pattern-anticipating expectations immediately subjected to critical review before assigning some plausibility evaluation.

Both overreliance on smartphone's retrieval abilities and instructions that mindlessly follow protocols distract from abductive tendencies to always look for more productive patterns. Black box thinking, so essential to the Great Conversation, never gets a chance to identify novel insights when at the moment of diagnosis, prognosis or teachable moment is subordinated to established algorithms. So there is no misunderstanding here; established algorithms are invaluable, and good thinkers often rely on them for good reason, namely, they usually work. But they must not be allowed to close out intuitions and cogent human abductions.

Information retrieval and the systematic updating of algorithms over time will never produce the dexterity of thinking that students need to address the challenges of the moment. Nor will teachers' overreliance on learned protocols model for students the dispositions and refinements of critical thinking. Students need teachers who can model intellectual dexterity. Lack of intellectual dexterity, and worse, adherence to poorly examined protocols, is analogous to the problem of overfitting the data in research.

"Over-fitting the data" roughly consists in following a model or protocol no matter how ill-fitting it proves to be (Christian & Griffiths, 2016). In practice, strict adherence to teaching protocols and dictated algorithms often leads students to blind spots in their reflective exercises.

This book focuses on showing teachers how to model a more refined instinct for depth and intellectual dexterity consistent with participation in the Great Conversation. This focus will alert new teachers to the dangers of overfitting models, protocols, and data that do not quite fit the immediate situation. The intellectual constructs people employ must be pragmatically responsive to the context and moment of inquiry. This responsiveness requires depth and intellectual dexterity. Depth and intellectual dexterity are best learned from participating in the Great Conversation prior to the moment of pedagogical decision.

As a teacher is himself or herself brought into the Great Conversation—especially as it applies to deliberations about pedagogical practice—he or she goes from being a merely competent teacher to being a teacher with promise for greatness. Previous errors in teaching strategies, as reflected upon during the Conversation, give teachers a chance to exploit past mistakes of both their own and others, on behalf of new learning. This Great Conversation-type of learning the teacher experiences is what is being lost from K–12 education. By learning to participate in such Great Conversation-type of learning himself or herself, the teacher is better suited to role-model such learning for his or her students.

IS EDUCATION BEST UNDERSTOOD AS COMPUTATIONAL EFFICIENCY?

Return to the example of medical education for a moment. Young residents can retrieve much information from their smartphone. Computational retrieval of information is a good thing. Students at every age—and not just medical students—should surely learn strategies for optimizing information retrieval practices. However, depth and intellectual dexterity require much more than efficiency in the retrieval of information to be pragmatically responsive to immediate context.

The retrieval of information cannot guarantee accuracy in every particular case, much less the apt deployment of information in either science or practical life. Each individual case of inquiry potentially contains some degree of novelty. Algorithms no matter how complex and elaborately organized are unlikely to account for all possibilities in apt fashion. For example, on average, 15% of all medical lab tests done in this country are in error. There are also many interfering factors that cause false positives and false negatives (Van Leeuwen, Poelhuis-Leth, & Bladh, 2016). As statistician Gary Feldman points out, the Kelly formula shows that similar ill-fitting of expectation occurs when test results are used by educators to identify student ability (as cited in Smith, 2016).

Computer algorithms calculate substantial amounts of information and give a best betting odds recommendation on what a patient suffers from and what prognosis is most likely (Christian & Griffiths, 2016). Similarly, there are standardized protocols for teaching students of a certain type, a specific subject. But is that all there is to medicine? Is that all there is to teaching excellence?

Physicians who are committed to health care and who are not simply administrators of medical treatment have to make decisions about an individual patient's quality of life, about this patient's hypochondria, about this patient's susceptibility to the "laying on of hands," and about other placebo strategies. Similarly, teachers who have a commitment to the individual student's success, and not the measurement of the class's success, must notice traits of each student that individuate him or her from the class norm.

When philosopher Robert Nozick (2001) was finishing his last book, *Invariances*, he was dying of stomach cancer. He asked doctors to use extreme measures to keep him alive until he finished the book. He also insisted they not give him painkillers in the morning so he would have a few hours of lucidity to write as best he could. Computers and the medical treatment options prescribed were not sufficient for addressing issues presented by Nozick's request. Computer algorithms cannot know what is most meaningful to a specific human being with his or her individuating dispositions and ambitions. Medical education preparing doctors for health care should prepare physicians for "Nozick challenges," which are more than just mere algorithms.

To take another example, self-driving cars employ learning algorithms to benefit from experience, presumably just as humans do. Millions of miles have been logged in cars from Google, Audi, Mercedes Benz, General Motors, and others. But driverless cars are still slamming on the brakes or weaving off the road because they cannot tell the difference between a plastic bag blowing across their path and a young child or squirrel crossing in front of them (Domingos, 2015). Obviously learning theory models for thinking machines are not sufficiently robust for capturing the essence of deep and dexterous human thinking. What to do?

Yet there is more. How do you teach a computational system to engage in moral reflection? Computational systems retrieve and sort through information, and, while sensors collect and aggregate observational data for processing, there are no sensors for detecting and processing human moral sensitivities. For example, imagine an auto accident is unavoidable. Should the driver act to protect passengers in the car or those outside the car? Can mere quantitative assessments settle such issues?

We noted previously the importance of individuating attention in teaching as much as in medicine. When considering the moral architecture that makes the Great Conversation so different from a mass protocol of information download, it is difficult not to recollect the writings of Martin Buber, a philosopher and Hasidic writer of years ago. He advised that communication intended to be meaningful addresses each listener as if he or she is all that matters, and the rest of the world recedes into the background for a few precious moments (Buber, 1958). Learning theory for standardized machines (and students) is ill-suited for engaging others in the depth and dexterous learning of the Great Conversation.

The Great Conversation has a distinct moral character that students learn from observing role-models rather than from rehearsed algorithms. The depth of the Conversation is driven by intense commitment to an earnest quest for truth and not the recovery of standardized information. The collaborative character of the Conversation focuses the participants' attention on their own and the others' character and moral commitment to the process. Computers, bulletin boards, and posters may project platitudes encouraging everyone to be tolerant and respectful of cultures different from their own, but speaking those platitudes is not the same as being genuinely committed to the values of tolerance and respect (Gardner, 2011).

In the moral domain, depth and intellectual dexterity show themselves when those who have participated in the Great Conversation know there is more to the moral world than reciting platitudes about recycling or global climate change. Students, who think deeply about moral responsibility to others, see beyond rote platitudes and may *feel* responsible for cutting the grass of a neighbor who is in the hospital with a heart attack or for taking a casserole to a neighboring household whose mother may be in the hospital with breast cancer.

Participation in the Great Conversation helps students recognize that moral development is about making the best of human nature. Education cannot settle for merely creating platitudes and protocols pertaining to the public good. Deeper thinking, assisted when needed by decision or game theory, and other critical thinking techniques make deep and dexterous moral thinking more accessible to all (Raeburn & Zollman, 2016).

Unfortunately, it can be very difficult to root out entrenched errors. For example, there are those educators who apparently think of children as simply egocentric creatures driven by self-interest. Such generalizations about students militate against leading them into ever-deeper moral reflection. Even though the "carrot or the stick" psychology has been discredited repeatedly by science, many practicing teachers continue to run their classrooms through regimens akin to the carrot or stick psychology (Sun, 2016).

Equally unfortunately, if the carrot or stick model is replaced by postulating human mental life viewed simply as computational modeling, we may again find ourselves going far astray (Poundstone, 1988). Replacing reinforcement schedules with programming algorithms is not a great advance. There is something to be gained by students automatically throwing refuse into appropriate recycling containers, but there is so much more they can and should learn about cooperative human engagement with others. This is when and where teachers need to think deeply themselves about their own roles in leading students to think deeply about what they may owe others.

WHAT IS THE IDEAL OF A GOOD EDUCATION?

More than ever before, education must develop students who think with the well-being of others in mind. One can be both a good thinker and wholly self-interested. But one can be a morally good thinker to the extent that one thinks of others. It would be impossible to participate fully in the Great Conversation and not consider the wisdom of such insight.

Patrick Henry's oft-repeated dictum, "United we stand, divided we fall," is more than potent political rhetoric. In fact, it matches what biologists now believe to be an asset evolution contrived in favor of every herd animal (Maestripieri, 2012). And, perhaps most important to the future teacher, it captures the energizing spirit of sustaining a lifelong commitment to the Great Conversation (Jackson, 2011).

Antiquated psychological learning strategies that focus on gadgets to increase recollection and access to facts are missing the most needed element of all for human education, namely, the need to think—to think objectively, to think rigorously, to evaluate exhaustively, to demand of self and others definitional clarity, to review, and finally to critique like a morally sensitive human being (Mlodinow, 2015).

A forthcoming revolution in psychology will take what we are learning about information processing, neuroscience, evolution, genetics, and so on and remake educational psychology. But if that revolution is to be truly productive, it must keep in mind human betterment, not just computational efficiency and information retrieval. It must focus our attention on developing morally sensitive humans (Sterelny, Joyce, Calcott, & Fraser, 2013).

At the cutting edge of computer science, few researchers are continuing to power their way through massive programs like IBM's chess-playing Big Blue in order to show how human minds work. Even parallel processing strategies, as Marvin Minsky pushed in the 1980s, have receded. Increasingly, learning algorithms are teaching computers to learn better as computers. There involves far less attention to mimicking how humans in fact think (Christian & Griffiths, 2016).

Do not get us wrong. There is still much of value to gain by building the next larger supercomputer and running financial management systems and government assets in such fashion. Parallel processing systems continue to pay dividends in time-sharing features akin to human organizational efforts. And, when it comes to looking to technology, software programs such as Watson are truly revolutionary and do seem to capture much more of what it means to think like a human (Baker, 2011). But not entirely.

Watson is a program using Bayesian statistics to determine the most likely apt response to a stimulus. Watson was designed to think like, and then better than, any human playing the game Jeopardy. It turns out that Jeopardy champions like Ken Jennings are rarely aware of the answer to a question prior to pressing the button. Instead, their brains seem to recognize a familiar intellectual neighborhood and initiate the psychomotor impulse while the brain continues to sink more deeply into the most apt response to the question at hand. This is exactly what Watson has learned to do (Baker, 2011).

Keep this in mind before we go on. Despite the dominance of high-stakes testing, educators are not in the business of preparing Jeopardy champions. The educator's challenge is far headier.

Watson is a learning program. Learning algorithms are now the software of choice-driving search engines such as Google, Bing, Yahoo!, and Amazon and self-driving cars. These computer programs are not deductively driven systems. They do not simply retrieve a compelling instruction, but rather they search for answers with the highest probability of being accurate (Christian &

Griffiths, 2016). Knowledge algorithms reach for the best bet given a set of input data. However, they are *unwitting* when it comes to the idea of seeking truth—truth of any kind.

Human minds run algorithms analogous to Watson and to the learning algorithms of most other search engines today. These algorithms are all driven by probabilistic search and recovery strategies (Christian & Griffiths, 2016). But there is more to human mental life. For example, humans have ambitions. In the Great Conversation, those ambitions often show up as hopeful excellence in the search for truth. Wholly computational minds are unwitting when it comes to truth or ambitions or emotions of any kind. The best they can do is come up with an operational simulacrum of human minds. Humans' deeper and dexterous thinking is not like theirs.

If an early hypothesis goes awry, humans incorporate that information probabilistically into a neurologically flexible and interactive learning system. The plasticity of this learning system (our brains) recalibrates in an instant and offers a next most likely suggestion. Computer scientists today are discovering learning software for machines that do more than catalog error and success rates. Like human minds, computational minds governed by learning algorithms compensate for errors of many types rather quickly.

Just adding code for each new fact does not improve machine intelligence any more than it improves human intelligence (Domingos, 2015). Oddly, however, much preparation for high-stakes testing aims at little more than cataloging of information and speed of retrieval.

So why do so many teachers still try to teach this way? More important, perhaps, is the fact that this information is likely to drive our responsiveness to the world than any self-conscious adherence to an algorithm (Gigerenzer & Todd, 1999). And, in addition, humans have a set of emotions and ambitions that affect their cognitions. Again, why do we persist in teaching as if all instructions can be broken down to a reinforcement schedule or a program-driven algorithm often captured in obsessively detailed rubrics? Teaching is neither mere behavioral training nor programming of a computational system. There is more to teaching than that, and now is the time to begin that further deep thinking about teaching.

We are not ruling out the importance of training or algorithmic learning altogether. In fact, one of the authors, Paul Wagner, is on record endorsing some drill and grill for students entering into new disciplines. The caveat, however, is that evidence of student reflective capacity must be recognized as a benchmark signaling the appropriate end of such practices and the initiation instead of a whole new angle on instruction that we call the Great Conversation of Humankind (Wagner, 2017).

In what follows, we have no intention of covering all angles of training, schooling, socialization, information retrieval technologies, or limited drill and grill strategies. Other than to say we think all of these have some place to varying degrees in the lives of learners. Nonetheless, there must be considered thought given to what deep and serious thinking about education tells us about what teachers should do and intend to do.

THE GREAT CONVERSATION OF HUMANKIND

In a nutshell, the Great Conversation takes place wherever participants engage one another's thinking respectfully and with an unmitigated focus on learning from error and pursuing the quest for truth (Wagner, Johnson, Fair, & Fasko, 2016, 2017). The Great Conversation is built on deliberative, deliberate, and critical self-reflection, as well as analysis of the competing views of others. The Great Conversation holds in reverence two questions: "How do you know?" and "What do you mean by the term___?" It uses these two questions to investigate claims and criticisms of other big questions about the world.

Given this definition of the Great Conversation of Humankind, other prescriptions implicitly follow. These prescriptions that direct the management of any authentic educational effort will come face-to-face with the ponderous question of "What is a 'good' education?"

Humans share in the same form of life with one another. We are, after all, but one species—cultural variants and all. David Hume believed that humans have an innate sense of sympathy for one another. Surely anyone who ever worked in a hospital nursery has seen infants only hours after birth cry out in sympathy when another infant cries in pain when having blood drawn. This cry of social sympathy typically agitates all the infants present, whereas a cry of hunger or a soiled diaper rarely elicits such universal responsiveness. Here is fodder for a big question: Do humans have a natural instinct to care about the well-being of one another? If they do, then why do they so often end up in hostile encounters with one another?

Big questions occur naturally to all humans. While humans share an inclination to raise big questions, there is considerable variance in the answers they consider. There is simply not one natural algorithm that leads inevitably to a single set of plausible answers (Hand, 2014). Computational processing is always a matter of cataloging and arranging. Humans and thinking machines both engage in such mental operations. But, in contrast to computers, humans share feelings, and their extensiveness and their cause cannot simply be algorithmically determined (Mazur, 2016).

For humans, feelings of wonderment and discovery excite the human spirit in ways inaccessible to machine intelligence or to intelligent systems limited to simple stimulus and response interactions. Neuroscientists can refer many feelings to the human limbic system, but locating the feelings in a part of the brain tells us nothing about what they mean to those who experience them (Sapolsky, 2017).

Learning what feelings mean is an important part of the Great Conversation. From the five-year-old to the fifty-five-year-old, human beings want answers to "Why do I feel this way now?"; "How should a person feel under the circumstances?"; and "Why are there feelings?" Speculations in answer to *why* questions must be refined through the questions "How do you know?" and "What do you mean by the term ___?"

To take another example, the heavens seem alive with activity, and to learn that we are on a bit of cosmic dust hurtling through space in the grip of our sun and in the further grip of a drifting galaxy is nothing short of fantastic. Humans are stunned by such facts, and young and old we want to know "Why?" The critical review within the Conversation ensures plausibility for some speculations while relieving us of unnecessary others. A computational mind has no excitation of wonderment. A neurological system may have a feel for such wonderment, but by itself it has no idea what to do with that feeling or what such a feeling might mean.

Education as the Great Conversation is an extraordinary and uniquely human experience, and teachers need to learn how to host the Conversation. In the context of a good education, teachers show students that such wonderment is a moment in which they should luxuriate, a moment for them to be uniquely and supremely human—capable of awe, reverence, and wonderment for all there is and all that we might come to understand. In the context of a good education, teachers invite reflection and encourage truth-seekers to ask why things are as they seem to be? Or what grounds are there for various hypotheses? And again, why are some hypotheses more intellectually satisfying to the human mind than others?

In the context of such robust educational authenticity, neither rapid retrieval of information nor algorithmic efficiency is good enough to meet the delight participants take in their shared and collective engagement. Computers do not need to respect each other. Biological organs have no idea what it means to respect other meat. Human participants alone recognize that in the Great Conversation, respect and other character-driven emotions are necessary to sustain progress.

Computational efficiency aims at benchmarking stopgap searches (Christian & Griffiths, 2016). Neurological efficiency aims at metabolic stability. Neither of these explains participatory success in the Great Conversation. Education lures humans together into this most extraordinary and exotic life practice. This surely is what each educator is aiming for as they consider the talents and duties necessary for being a good teacher. In the simplest of terms, a good education vis-a-vis good teaching leads students into a lifetime of appreciation for and participation in the Great Conversation of Humankind.

GOOD TEACHERS

What counts as a good education is a concept now roughly at hand. Keeping things as simple as possible, good teachers can be defined as guardians of the Great Conversation. Of course, now it becomes imperative to define what it means to be a guardian of the Conversation. Phillip Jackson (2012) describes education in rather lofty terms, but in the end, he proposes something along the lines of Deweyan pragmatism, a perfect fit for understanding the Great Conversation.

For present purposes, suffice it to say that guardians of the Great Conversation, teachers, are those who are dedicated to keeping the Conversation alive and flourishing. They

1. allocate enough time for deep learning,
2. interact with their students, and
3. provide appropriate selection of examples and nonexamples (Sugar & Tindal, 1993).

These behaviors are exhibited in effective teachers, and they are enhanced, we propose, through the use of scripts.

We also propose that the use of scripts will provide for a school climate that is conducive to learning. In fact, school climate that is conducive to learning is an important characteristic of an effective school (Edmonds, 1979). Further, Adams (1993) notes that effective schools provide for teacher-student interaction that enhances students' engagement in learning. Thus, by using scripts in the classroom, students' critical thinking skills will improve, which will subsequently improve a school's effectiveness.

Long before there was anything such as teacher certification, there were guardians of the Conversation. Socrates comes to mind as one who lived his commitment to the Conversation day by day and who even sacrificed his life rather than shrink from the principles that make the Conversation great. Socrates was all about addressing big questions and critically evaluating the best arguments to wherever they lead. Socrates feared no question or any discovery. He was a paradigmatic role-model as a guardian. Will you be that guardian when you teach?

The example of Socrates serves well as a prototype for the idea of a guardian of the Great Conversation. Anyone who was willing to entertain difficult questions, and follow where the collective effort to understand led, was welcomed by Socrates into the Conversation. This was good teaching. Socrates asked provocative questions—not to ridicule other participants but to lead everyone to query what seemed missing from any presented judgment or hypothesis. This too is good teaching. If these ideas energize a person, then he or she should think about a career of teaching.

There was more to Socrates's role-modeling. Socrates was relentless in his pursuit of truth. And as psychologist Albert Bandura so often insisted, it is through role-modeling that teachers have the greatest effect on the learners (Bandura, 1976). Socrates lived to an old age but never gave up on participation in the Conversation. He was truly a lifelong learner. Socrates used what he recalled to search for further truth and not simply rehearse what he already knew. His students saw all that in him. Will your students see all that in you?

In short, the idea of a teacher as guardian of the Great Conversation can be summed as follows:

1. Teachers should do all they can to lure students into universal participation in the Conversation.
2. Teachers are hosts of the Conversation. They should make every participant feel comfortable and welcome.
3. Teachers should draw attention to the big questions if participants become distracted by the mundane.
4. Teachers should acknowledge what seems to be plausibly known but always with an eye to following up with questions about how it is known, why it is important, and what is the meaning of what is known to the Conversation.
5. Teachers should bravely model respect and insist that it always be in place for every participant and every earnestly offered argument or hypotheses.
6. Teachers should consistently draw attention to semantic clarity to ensure optimal understanding of views by all participants.
7. They should be patient and always encourage students to elaborate further on how it is that they know something that they think they know.
8. Teachers should sustain the Conversation by never closing the door on discussion, never indicating that the matter is settled once and for all.
9. Teachers should understand the challenge of liberating students from bias and prejudice and handicapping intellectual habits in order to extend each student's own sense of autonomy.
10. Teachers should show that participation in the Conversation can be a model of moral communion within a community.

TEACH GOOD THINKING

When teachers effectively host the Great Conversation, they are of necessity teaching students the elements and strategies of good thinking. Good thinkers are moved initially by the fostering of wonderment. Wonderment is something evolution equipped humans with long before anything called a teacher or a school ever existed. Wonderment and learning are instinctual. But these instincts may be extinguished by bad teaching and by media distractions.

Evolutionary psychologists have warned that the key question in motivating students is not "How do you motivate them?" Evolution already addressed that (Wiley, 2015). Rather the key critical question for practicing educators is to ask: "What are we doing to drive the natural instinct of wonderment and learning out of students?"

Learning is an innate instinct that benefits from systematic development (Mlodinow, 2015). That instinct is best developed by creating a learning ambience; call it a community of learners. The successful community of inquirers collectively challenges and rewards each participant for figuring things out. There are a number of qualities exhibited by those who are good thinkers:

1. Good thinkers learn to quickly take stock of where their deliberations are beginning.
2. Good thinkers take inventory of what they presumably know, what they are ready to assume, and what knowledge and assumptions they may be relying on.
3. Good thinkers know there is more to good thinking than just guessing a right answer.
4. Good thinkers aim at answers that are demonstratively plausible.
5. Good thinkers seek justification for apparently sound conclusions.
6. Good thinkers are eager to learn strategies that optimize inference-making reliability.
7. Good thinkers are wary that there are many fallacies and other flaws that can infect any carelessly pursued inquiry.
8. Good thinkers focus on moving away from avoidable error. In short, good thinkers are truth-seekers.
9. Good thinkers are respectful of and open-minded toward critical review by others.
10. Good thinkers seek out criticism and contributions by any and every fellow participant in the Great Conversation.

Good thinking is the heart of the process in the Great Conversation. Good thinkers are the product. But neither good thinkers nor good thinking is self-sustaining without return to the context and practice of the Great Conversation.

In the chapters that follow, teachers and future teachers will be challenged to think more about the details of good thinking. Those chapters will show how a focus on the process and intellectual side of pedagogical practice adds a dimension to teaching potency seldom found in training programs that focus on little more than optimal retrieval of information.

This dimension of a teacher-training program is about intellectual processing, about figuring out the world, and about engaging it as effectively as natural human attributes allow. Some of those attributes are an instinctual sense of cooperation and sympathy for the well-being of others in addition to modest self-interest in one's own well-being. This approach amplifies individual autonomy but does not lead to nihilism but rather to collaboration. The most effective intellectual processing relies on thinkers *thinking together*, both creating and critically reviewing one another's ideas.

This approach is aimed at enabling teachers to create an ambience conducive to rigorous thinking by their students on the basis of the students' own experience. This sounds lofty, but in a rough and ready way, it means simply enabling the teachers to think more deeply about teaching and, through practice, to help them role-model deep thinking for their students.

Teachers cannot give to their students what they themselves have not developed. In the pages ahead, and especially as teachers begin using scripts with one another, they will learn to think about teaching in ways far exceeding any mundane approach to job training. As they become deeper thinkers, they will be in a better position to take advantage of those rare teachable moments in their classrooms, moments that will help their students enter into the Great Conversation of Humankind.

Chapter 2

Current Realities

The Programme for International Student Assessment (Simon, 2013) consistently shows the United States doing poorly in science, technology, engineering, and mathematics (STEM) subjects compared to other major industrial countries, as well as countries like Estonia, Singapore, and Vietnam. The United States once was considered a leader in education. Lately, however, test results seem to show the United States lagging behind in STEM subjects. What exactly do these measurements reflect? The Common Core curriculum and high-stakes testing (also referred to as accountability testing) have, in one way or another, been created in response to lagging comparative test scores (Hacker, 2016).

HISTORY OF THE COMMON CORE CURRICULUM

The public school system has continually sought new and improved methods, strategies, and professional practices to improve the public education system. Beginning in 1983, with the publication of the report *A Nation at Risk*, the federal government began to involve itself in public education by legislating the Elementary and Secondary Education Act (ESEA). ESEA ensured public schools federal funding tied to federal mandates (Groen, 2012).

ESEA was reauthorized in 2001 with the No Child Left Behind (NCLB) legislation. Curriculum and instructional coherence became a major focus of the education system. The vision of coherence included common curricula, instructional strategies, and instructional materials, as well as aligned assessments (Polikoff, Porter, & Smithson, 2011). The thinking being that if all children were taught the same curriculum using the same materials and the same strategy, they all would do well on the aligned assessment.

NCLB did help improve the school system by requiring proof that students were learning. However, reducing the proof of students' learning to a single performance on a standardized test was problematic. "It is, however, the testing regime required by NCLB that has most profoundly altered the curriculum and pedagogy since its passage in 2001" (Groen, 2012, p. 8).

Unfortunately, according to Linda Darling-Hammond (2007), this greater emphasis on testing has led to an increase in the number of children being left behind, especially those lower-performing students. These were precisely the students that NCLB was supposed to help.

Lower-performing students who do graduate from high school and enroll in community colleges are often placed into developmental courses; the highest frequency of placements occurs in developmental math courses, such as basic math. Unless these students are successful in these basic math courses, they cannot progress to college-level coursework. Unfortunately, very high percentages of students placed in developmental math courses never progress beyond those courses and therefore never realize their goals in higher education. Inability to succeed in basic math courses may present the most significant obstacle to this population's success in college (Secolsky et al., 2016, p. 1).

Even with these curriculum changes, the National Center for Education Statistics (NCES) reported that about 40% of the U.S. population who graduated from high school needed remedial coursework before taking college-level courses. In addition, the NCES reported that only 30% of those students earned a postsecondary degree or certificate (Hain & Piper, 2016; Wirt et al., 2004).

In a further effort to improve the education system, in 2009, the National Governors' Association Center for Best Practices and the Council of Chief State School Officers began to develop a set of Common Core State Standards (henceforth referred to as the Common Core) for students in all states. Although the federal government, with bipartisan support, encouraged the development of a common national curriculum, it was not involved in the actual development of the standards. The standards were designed to be rigorous, robust, and relevant to the real world in order to fully prepare American students for success in college, careers, and the global economy (Campbell-Whatley, Dunaway, & Hancock, 2016).

When the standards had been reviewed and validated by all stakeholders, the standards were released for voluntary adoption by the states. Forty-five states, two territories, and the District of Columbia chose to adopt the newly released standards (Center for Public Education, 2013). Alaska, Nebraska, Texas, and Virginia chose not to adopt the new standards, while Minnesota adopted only the English/Language Arts Standards.

The standards aim to provide clear and consistent guidelines for administrators, educators, and parents to ensure that all students are prepared for the future. They focus on critical thinking and problem solving, as well as writing and technology skills, that students will need for success in college, their career, and the global economy.

Campbell-Whatley et al. (2016) outline five reasons why common standards are so important for the United States. First, other countries (e.g., Finland and Singapore) with more successful student outcomes have a required national curriculum (Hancock, 2011; Ministry of Education, Singapore, 2016). This is believed to be a major reason these countries' students are so successful (Manley & Hawkins, 2010).

An additional reason for common core standards is that new skills are required in the present and future workforce. Employers are requiring more critical thinking and problem-solving skills in their employees to fit with the ever-changing world. A third reason is that participating states will have aligned curriculum and expectations. Students moving from one participating state to another can expect the same requirements, thus decreasing the chance they will confront drastic changes in curriculum and instruction.

A fourth reason is that educators from all participating states can collaborate on lesson plans, assessments, and teaching strategies. And, finally, built into the standards is a strong emphasis on a research component and on media literacy skills. Both are critical for success in our changing world.

However, there is dissent. In their article in *Radical Pedagogy*, Chomsky and Robichaud (2014) argue strongly against a standardized curriculum. They contend that "standardized educational practices represent an attack on humanistic and critical education, as they are politically made to annihilate students and teachers creativity, individuality and autonomy." Furthermore, they are concerned that this will encourage "teaching to the test" that limits how students' knowledge and skills will be assessed—primarily by paper and pencil, multiple-choice tests.

IMPLEMENTATION OF THE COMMON CORE CURRICULUM STANDARDS

Another issue arises because, ideally, the implementation of the Common Core would be standardized in all states, but, in reality, not only were states given the choice to adopt the standards, but they were also given discretion in the implementation strategy. Unfortunately, information has been scarce since the adoption of the standards regarding any sharing of mathematics resources. However, relationships have been developed among the states for sharing resources in the English Language Arts area (Zubrzycki, 2017). That being said, Zubrzycki (2017) reported that only "17.5% of the resources shared by states were concrete instructional resources, while most materials shared were conceptual documents about standards and research."

During 2011 and 2012, participating states and territories began their own implementation processes for "reviewing, adopting, and (in some states) ratifying the adoption of the Common Core State Standards. In each case, after reviewing the new standards, state boards of education members, governors, legislators, and/or chief state school officers took action to replace their existing standards with the Common Core State Standards" (Polikoff, 2014, p. 19). Each participating state and territory implemented the Common Core Standards using their own strategy and their own timeline.

ASSESSMENT AND THE COMMON CORE CURRICULUM STANDARDS

To verify the impact and ensure success of the Common Core Standards implementation, assessment became an important component of the new curriculum. Interestingly, one of the characteristics of high-performing schools reported in the past decade is that their curriculum, instruction, and assessment are aligned with state standards (Shannon & Bylsma, 2007). In regard to the Common Core Standards, ideally, states would work together to create a common assessment, thus ensuring an equitable comparison between the states. In reality, however, as with implementation, states were given a lot of discretion in how the new standards would be assessed.

As mentioned previously, forty-five states, two territories, and the District of Columbia have legislated commitment to the Core Curriculum Standards, thus catapulting test performance as a measure of good education to the forefront. The data obtained from these accountability/high-stakes tests have an impact on administrators, teachers, and students. For example, students' scores may affect their being promoted from one grade to another (Slavin, 2015). An unfortunate problem is that the Common Core Standards are tied to assessments that are still in development and that must be given on computers many schools do not have.

Another problem is that all this continuous testing tends to, as Sternberg (2016) noted, "improve the skills on which students are tested" (p. 67). The students practice taking tests, with test-taking strategies taught by their teachers. These strategies facilitate the students' retrieval of the content tested, which are typically basic facts (Williams, 1998). None of these techniques, however, promotes critical thinking. In fact, Chomsky and Robichaud (2014) state that methods that teach to the test are "deadening to the human mind."

Along similar lines, Darling-Hammond (2007) stated:

> Critics claim that the law's focus on complicated tallies of multiple-choice test scores has dumbed down the curriculum, fostered a drill and kill approach to teaching, mistakenly labeled successful schools as failing, driven teachers and middle-class students out of public schools and harmed special education students and English-language learners through inappropriate assessments and efforts to push out low-scoring students in order to boost scores. (p. 4)

Finally, although the major goal of federal and state high-stakes testing policies was to improve schools, "the theory of action undergirding this approach suggests that by tying negative consequences (e.g., public exposure, external takeover) to standardized test performance, teachers and students in low performing schools will work harder and more effectively, thereby increasing what students learn" (Nichols, Glass, & Berliner, 2012, p. 2). But because of the negative consequences, teachers feel compelled to train their students for these tests.

Interestingly, there is no research or experience to date to justify the extravagant claims made for the ability of these standards to ensure that every child will graduate from high school and college and be career ready (Karp, 2013/2014). By all accounts, the new Common Core tests will be considerably harder than current state assessments, leading to a sharp drop in scores and proficiency rates (Karp, 2013/2014), as well as students being promoted.

With regard to accountability testing and curriculum alignment with implementation of the standards, Boostrom (2015) pointed out that "the price of this rhetorically coherent system is the surrender of any hope for a transformative education that encourages openness of mind and creativity of thought" (p. 85). Boostrom also suggested that standards-based curricula hinder critical thinking. This is echoed by Landsman and Gorski (2007), who identify five myths that contribute to inflicting a standardized, test-driven curriculum on students. They suggest that we need to teach critical thinking skills in our schools and that we should not accept the myth that "teaching critical thinking and social consciousness is political" (p. 42).

An example of the implementation of the Common Core Standards is reported by Boostrom (2015) when he asserts that the Indiana Department of Education (IDE) in implementing the Common Core Standards assumed that what "students learn is what we intend to teach them" (p. 92).

As with other states that adopted the Common Core Standards, the IDE used standardized tests as accountability measures to determine if students met their achievement goals. Boostrom's concern is that the IDE's curriculum "exists external to students and is something to which students must be fitted" (p. 93), and, the emphasis on content, the promotion of critical thinking skills, is missing.

Some see a positive trend, in that, according to Moore and Stanley (2010), state accountability tests "are increasingly emphasizing thinking and problem solving" (as cited in Smith & Szymanski, 2013, p. 17). However, we must consider *what kind of thinking* is being encouraged in these standards and, subsequently, what kind of thinking the students are capable of doing (Boostrom, 2015).

Common Core Standards, when coupled with standardized accountability testing, appear to not promote critical thinking in K–12 students. The challenge for colleges/schools of education is to teach preservice teachers both how to improve their own critical thinking skills (Landsman & Gorski, 2007) and how to stimulate their future students' critical thinking under Common Core Standards. However, the Association of American Colleges and Universities (AACU, 2002) reported that few preservice teachers were taught how to develop and use their own critical thinking skills.

The question, then, for teacher educators is how best to foster growth in their students' critical thinking skills. Perhaps educators should be confident that, as Minnich (2003) stated, "If we can teach writing across the curriculum, surely we can and should also teach thinking across the curriculum" (p. 24). The aim is to enhance preservice teachers' critical thinking skills so that they can make good decisions (S. K. Johnson, 2012) and then facilitate good decision making in their students. One way to do this is through the use of scripts to promote classroom discussion, but encouraging university instructors in colleges/schools of education to modify their methods of teaching will not be easy.

Nevertheless, we must move forward since there is much about a good education that does not reduce to simple mastery of multiple test items over a narrowly contrived curriculum (Koretz, 2008). Instead, we need to focus on developing problem-solving and critical thinking skills in students. One sign of progress is that there have been many innovative and productive interdisciplinary instructional programs, especially in the STEM subjects, that have led to great benefits for students and the communities in which they live (Koretz, 2008).

THE CHALLENGE OF KNOWLEDGE "SILOS"

Over the years, many educators focused on creating disciplines or "silos" of specific subjects. These silos encourage teachers to teach subjects in isolation. The Pythagorean theorem, for example, fits into the mathematics silo.

The law of supply and demand fits into the social studies silo, evolution into the biology silo, and so on.

"However, society does not function in distinct categories, and the creation of separate disciplines discourages recognition of the unity of knowledge" (Mei, 2009, p. 40). Students learn that subjects do not overlap and spend twelve years studying and being assessed on each subject separately. Eventually, they are unable to see the big picture of the integration of knowledge, leading "to limited understanding and narrow-mindedness" (Mei, 2009, p. 40).

A curriculum of knowledge silos tends to separate the retrieval of information from its ultimate function, which presumably is to promote more effective thinking practices. Particularly disturbing about a focus on retrieving information from knowledge silos is the fact that there are smartphones, computers, and a host of powerful search engines available to most students. The ready availability of information seems to cheapen the utility of information retrieval in the eyes of many students, and so the cry of "Why do we have to learn this?" is perhaps louder than ever before.

It seems that information is there for the asking, but of far more utility is the skill it takes to evaluate the validity and reliability of the information collected. Yet high-stakes testing all but ignores such critical thinking skills. Instead, it seeks to identify students' ability to retrieve information. Oddly, information retrieval is a skill that students' smartphones do better than students could ever hope to master.

As a consequence of this practice, important questions are omitted such as:

1. Why do you want this information?
2. How will this information help you frame or solve a problem?
3. Are you prepared to organize the information you recover to optimize the utility of an emerging solution to some problem?

These questions are often not addressed in any fashion on these high-stakes tests, and that, unfortunately, means the questions (and their answers) are not focused on in classrooms.

Answers to questions such as these will nearly always involve some interdisciplinary scaffolding, and yet interdisciplinary scaffolding is becoming ever more uncommon—save for some special programs for the gifted (programs that are regrettably being cut because of funding issues in many states) or save for some charter schools.

Unfortunately, the Common Core continues this trend of knowledge silos being divided into two main silos—English Language Arts/Literacy Standards and Mathematics Standards. These silos stack information for retrieval within the well-defined curriculum selected for standardized test score improvement. Each silo tests according to a catalogue of stacked information. Students are to show they can recognize and retrieve information provided to them from a specific silo.

For a variety of reasons such as overemphasizing STEM (Hacker, 2016) and inept statistical reasoning, which fails to distinguish between performance and the regression to the mean interfering with telltale data (Smith, 2014), the benefits of STEM initiatives and critical thinking programs are not recognized for their positive contributions.

TROUBLE FINDING THE "TEACHABLE MOMENT"

The heavy reliance on adhering to the mandated, siloed Common Core interferes with many spontaneous opportunities in a classroom where students' natural interest and learning can be capitalized on by the teacher. Known as the "teachable moment," it is an extremely powerful learning opportunity where learning is exciting and natural.

A teachable moment could be as simple as "a question from a student, an object a student brought to class, unanticipated results in a lab investigation, a misconception, or an opportunity to connect what students are learning in science to other subjects or real-world events" (Bigelow, 2010). This spontaneous learning offers opportunities to connect content areas to real-world current events, offer a chance to help our students explore complex situations that demand that they think critically, and consider other perspectives (Mei, 2009). This is also an opportunity to introduce scripts in a content area to stimulate critical thinking.

Unfortunately, teachers are generally required to adhere to a "if it is Tuesday, we are teaching decimals" mentality. The discretion to reteach a topic when needed or cover a topic in more depth is lost in order to stay on the district-mandated calendar. Education has become focused on covering the required information rather than teaching children and making sure they learn. Consequently, many teachers feel their professional judgment and creativity are no longer trusted or valued, and they leave the field.

Teachers who remain work desperately to teach all the required standards in the required time frame and to still find time to enrich the students' education. However, for many of them, education has had to become a drill and memorization activity to prepare for high-stakes, multiple-choice tests. True, deep learning rarely occurs. Instructional time to allow students the opportunity to solve problems and think critically is rare.

This emphasis has created a generation of students who ask questions such as, "How long does it need to be?" "What do you want it to look like?" and so on. They are extremely uncomfortable with open-ended assignments and expect to be given an example of "what you want." Then, as a teacher, you can expect to receive multiple copies of the example. From time to time, a teacher may receive a truly creative submission, but it is a rarity. Education was once the avenue to becoming a good citizen, preparing for an occupation, and learning about the world. Today, however, education seems to be about preparing for a high-stakes, multiple-choice test.

A RAY OF HOPE? THE EVERY STUDENT SUCCEEDS ACT

The passage in 2015 of the Every Student Succeeds Act (ESSA), supplanting NCLB, may present an occasion for rethinking the nearly exclusive reliance on high-stakes, multiple-choice testing to assess and hold accountable teachers and schools. Thus, Linda Darling-Hammond (2017) asserts:

> These new opportunities are critically important because current test in the U.S. are focused almost exclusively on low-level skills of recall and recognition. Consequently, they do not provide incentives for teaching the more complex skills students increasingly need to succeed in the rapidly evolving U.S. society and economy. (p. 2)

But because of ESSA, Darling-Hammond avers:

> The door is now open for educators to use most comprehensive systems to evaluate students' academic progress. These systems could include components such as (1) performance tasks to be performed as a part of tests, (2) curriculum-embedded tasks to assess more complex skills, (3) and portfolios or collections of evidence. (p. 3)

The historical irony in this situation is that a number of states were moving toward such comprehensive systems of evaluation in the 1990s, and those movements practically came to a standstill with the passage of NCLB.

If the present situation gives us an opportunity to revisit how we assess student learning, at the same time, it opens a door for more thoughtful ways to evaluate teachers as professionals. For example, on the basis of extensive research, Lerner and Tetlock (1999) stressed that "accountability is not a unitary phenomenon" (p. 255). They identified four different factors underlying practices of accountability, including the mere presence of another person, the clarity that what someone says or does can be linked to them personally, evaluations involving some normative ground rules and consequences, and finally situations in which participants anticipate that they be required to give reasons to explain what they say or do.

This becomes the basis for proposals like that of Gill, Lerner, and Meosky (2016), which recognizes that we have stressed *outcome based accountability* and, by contrast, have used much less frequently accountability processes involving *reason giving* or *the presence of another*. Indeed, Gill et al. worry that "aggressive rule-based accountability employing highly scripted instructional programs, while they may have their uses, are unlikely to promote excellence in teaching particularly for deep and complex curricular material" (p. 62).

Finally, a number of states have used or are in the process of creating systems to evaluate schools, often by using criteria to assign a single-letter grade A to F to the whole school. There is considerable interest in how such systems operate and whether they will have the sort of positive consequences envisaged by their architects (Valant, 2017). Understandably, standardized state test results often play a large role in such systems, but here is an illustration why some people are hesitant to embrace them.

Consider the case of a state which is in the process of creating a system and which reports that preliminary results show a correlation between performance on state tests and the percentage of economically disadvantaged students that is strongly negative at −0.70 (Texas Education Agency, 2016, p. E-3). Next consider teaching the four elementary schools in a small district where the percentages of economically disadvantaged students are 67.2%, 61.3%, 73.4%, and 65.5%. It would not be much of a surprise to see that the respective grades for the schools are D, F, F, and D. It is not hard to imagine how concerns about equity may quickly arise.

Under ESSA many commentators see an opportunity as one says "to create school rating systems that are simple, clear, and fair" (Aldeman, 2016). Aldeman proposes a model accountability system that uses test scores to flag campuses that may need attention but then relies on professional inspectors to investigate on-site and make suggestions for improvement. Moreover, some observers think that ESSA may provide leverage to address concerns about equity, including equity of resources available (Cook-Harvey, Darling-Hammond, Lam, Mercer, & Roc, 2016).

So the point is that states appear to be moving away from a near-exclusive reliance on standardized test results for evaluating students, their teachers, and their schools. This could enhance the prospects for recognizing successfully teaching students to think in the dexterous ways required for them to participate in the communities in which the Great Conversation takes place.

SO WHERE DO WE GO FROM HERE?

One solution is to better prepare preservice teachers to the current realities of public school education. In preservice teacher education, there must be a concerted effort to enhance these students' knowledge and skills to promote critical thinking in our K–12 students to better prepare them for the realities of the twenty-first century's requirements for higher education and the workforce. We suggest that, by using scripts to promote classroom discussion of meaningful issues, teacher educators will succeed in this endeavor. (See Wagner et al. [2016] and Wagner et al. [2017] for examples of scripts that can be used with students from third through twelfth grades.) It is an important ethical behavior on the part of colleges/schools of education.

Chapter 3

Values and Critical Thinking

UNDERSTANDING EDUCATOR DUTIES

If you want to find a duty-free zone, education is not the right place for you. The whole idea of education originated in and continues to be associated with the idea of values and human betterment. Think about it.

People can be taught to do heinous acts, such as torture an animal. People can be taught to read, write, do arithmetic, appreciate art, have sex education, and more. Teachers teach these subjects, attitudes, and skills rather than how to torture an animal because teachers value these skills and subjects over teaching behaviors such as torturing animals. Such decisions are culturally laden, but they are also reflective of individual moral sensitivities.

Culture influences and may even determine many habits of mind, fashion, business, social activity, and so on. Culture determines much of what is in the curriculum of an educational system. While all that may be true, you are still largely responsible for your decision to teach, what you teach, and how you go about teaching (Wagner, 1996).

Dating back across millennia, the decision you and others made to become teachers is based on your values and the moral commitment you associate with being a teacher. Presumably most people decide to become teachers because they value developing students through learning, reading, writing, arithmetic, and reasoning of all sorts. People who train to become teachers do so because, implicitly, they believe the world is better off by welcoming students into the Great Conversation.

In short, the task of becoming a teacher centers on the value a teacher places on welcoming students into the Great Conversation. Teachers are the hosts of the Great Conversation. They are duty-bound to ensure the Great Conversation remains open to all.

COMPLIANCE AND PERSONAL VALUES

There have been traditional duties accumulating around the role of teacher since the first teachers were identified in earliest antiquity. This tradition of the profession of teaching, like the tradition of the other three historic professions of lawyering, preaching, and doctoring, should supersede the duties imposed by any local legislation (Wagner & Lopez, 2010).

As an example of professional ethics trumping local legislation, consider an example from the profession of medicine. Japanese and German military officers who were doctors were convicted of war crimes following World War II for the hideous experiments they did to captives. Although the doctors claimed they were under orders from their superiors, international war-crimes courts held that their responsibility as medical professionals and as human beings superseded their obligation to obey their commanding officers.

In a similar vein, some educators have argued, for instance, that, while governments may impose penalties on illegal immigrants for unlawfully crossing onto their sovereign soil, teachers should not turn away those who show up at the doorstep willing to learn, any more than doctors should turn away someone needing immediate medical care (Wagner & Lopez, 2010).

In addition to duties imposed by tradition, teachers have individual moral commitments. What should be done when individual moral commitments run afoul of law or district policy? In the legal profession, it has become commonplace to distinguish between personal morality and legal ethics. Legal ethics are those dos and don'ts that the profession has established as guidelines for appropriate professional conduct. Failure to comply with a legal ethic may be morally right in some sense, but the attorney who fails to be in compliance with legal ethics can be censured, reprimanded, or even disbarred.

The same is true for doctors, preachers, and teachers. Consider an example from each profession. A doctor may see a patient suffering with no chance of ever recovering a reasonable quality of life. Yet the doctor in most states must resuscitate the patient until such time as an immediate family member signs papers acknowledging that it is his or her relative's wish not to suffer any further. If the doctor fails to resuscitate without the family's consent, the doctor is out of compliance and subject to some legal sanction.

In 1992, a preacher in Pearland, Texas, was reading scripture in front of a Planned Parenthood Center. He was arrested for disturbing the peace. Certainly it was very disconcerting for some of the women to be going into the center with this fellow out front reading from his Bible. The judge forbade the preacher to read from the Bible again within a thousand feet of the center. His superior directed him to follow the law. He did not. He thought it was his duty to violate the law and ignore his superior. He was jailed for thirty days and fired. Compliance versus personal morality. Did he do right or wrong?

In one of the nation's largest cities, an inner-city school with 93% of students making the school eligible for Title I funding and with 88% of students representing a single minority, an elementary-grade student had a severe asthma attack. She didn't have her medicine, and her parents couldn't be reached. The school called 911. Fifteen minutes later there was still no ambulance. The school nurse told the principal, "She isn't going to make it if she doesn't get help right away." What should the principal do?

He called 911 again. District policies and the state code of educator ethics prohibit educators from ever putting a student in a private vehicle. Yet knowing this and seeing that after another five minutes no ambulance arrived, the principal put the little girl in his personal car and drove to the nearest hospital. The doctors there said he probably saved the girl's life. Compliance versus personal morality. Did he do right or wrong?

What if the girl died in his car while he was driving her to the hospital? What if, in addition, an ambulance had pulled up to the school minutes after he left? (In fact an ambulance did not show up for nearly another twenty minutes.) In either of these outcomes, both the principal and the school could be sued by the girl's parents. So, why and how, should that matter? Compliance versus personal morality. Did he do right or wrong?

Addressing this challenge is not a matter of retrieving the right information. The principal had all available information. He could answer all test items on a statewide professional ethics test for educators. But what about making the correct real-world decision? Did he get it right? Did he get it wrong? Here is a case where compliance restrictions and personal morality are both centered on presumably right-minded intentions, yet they seem to conflict. What ought a responsible principal to do?

There is nothing to turn to in cases such as these beyond what we are calling the law of figuring things out. The law of figuring things out (hereafter LFTO) prescribes assembling all relevant information and then subjecting these to slow-thinking intellectual strategies that seem best suited to revealing an optimally plausible answer. Neither fast thinking nor any kind of guesswork or feel of the situation will prove to be consistently better at responding to such real-world challenges.

You cannot call on your smartphone assistant for the proper answer to these moral versus assigned responsibilities. You cannot look up the answer in a book. You cannot call or text a moral genius for the answer. In the end you must think very carefully and skillfully to arrive at a well-justified and plausible answer that deserves your commitment. Answers are well justified when from initial assumptions and observations, careful reasoning leads to support of one conclusion over other alternatives. An answer is plausible when it seems to fit the challenge with no outstanding flaws on reasoning or informational content.

We are not encouraging you to "willy-nilly" abandon compliance restrictions governing educator behavior whenever you feel like it. The point here is the fundamental fact that in the end, in that moment of decision, you are always the final decision maker. When there are competing claims on your genuine commitment to acting in right-minded fashion, for example, a conflict between compliance and personal morality, you will have to do some excellent figuring. Reflecting on such decisions along with others in the Great Conversation may help when the moments of difficult moral decisions inevitably arrive.

COMMUNITY OF LEARNING

The ability to reflect about one's decisions is best developed in a *community of learning*, that is, a community that encourages *inquiry*. So it is important for any adult, and especially a teacher, to think together with other critical thinkers in a "community" (Brookfield, 2003). One way to develop this sense of a reflective community is for leaders to role-model active participation for those new to the particular learning community. This role-modeling requires participants to collaborate in decision making with one another (Chickering & Gamson, 1987).

In this book we explain how and why learning communities using scripts can sharpen their skills of figuring things out through participation in a learning community. Participation in the community will and should lead to some cognitive dissonance. There will, as Brookfield (2003) observes, be times participants must endure some confusion. This confusion is inevitable when struggling to secure razor-sharp focus on distressing intellectual challenges. Critical thinking eases the struggle productively.

Individuals in a learning community serve as both learner and teacher when communication is open and collaborative. In a learning community, students cultivate "metacognitive awareness and ability" (Garrison, 2016, p. 23). Metacognition is roughly a matter of thinking about thinking, and since in a learning community, participants promote and challenge one another's thinking, this practice leads to enhanced metacognition.

In particular, it is important that preservice teachers be involved in deep thinking before they enter their professional roles so they can model the type of thinking desperately needed in the nation's classrooms. And it is important that they come to grips with some of the most intractable problems of teaching today.

Thus, as students, preservice teachers need to learn from participation in a learning community where they enhance the community's robustness by making their own contributions. And so it is that preservice teachers through the use of the scripts at the end of this book can learn from modeling and listening to one another how best to consider the challenges they will one day face in teaching.

SCHOOL CLASSROOMS AS LEARNING COMMUNITIES, AS COMMUNITIES OF INQUIRY

If preservice teachers have the benefit of participating in learning communities during their education, then they will be better able to create learning communities or communities of inquiry in their own classrooms. A result will be classrooms that because they are communities of inquiry (COI) will enhance students' critical thinking abilities (Kuhn, 2015). A COI-centered classroom exemplifies a learning environment where higher-order or critical thinking is valued and developed.

A shared perspective on developing COIs in school classrooms is found in Cleghorn (2002) and Lipman (2003). For example, Lipman states that a COI "attempts to follow the inquiry where it leads rather than being penned in the boundary lines of disciplines" (p. 15). Of course, as Garrison notes (2016), this may not always lead to agreement among the group members.

In order for a COI to nurture critical thinking, collaboration is an essential element in a COI (Garrison, 1991). And, as Garrison, Anderson, and Archer (2000) note, in a COI the "teacher models critical discourse and constructively critiques contributions [of the students] in order to promote higher-order learning outcomes" (as cited in Barber, 2011, p. 7). It is our conviction that carefully crafted scripted discussions ensure *active participation* both by the teachers and students alike (Barber, 2011).

In facilitating discussions around scripts, it is important for instructors to ask abstract open-ended questions. However, not all preservice teachers initially have the skills to ask these types of questions, so this is something that must be modeled in their education now as they prepare for their role one day as teachers. So, for example, skills in asking abstract questions will be developed in them as they participate with their instructor in the scripted discussions contained in this book.

Thinking collaboratively stimulates innovation in thinking, that is, critico-creative thinking, and therefore learning that is meaningful. Collaborative thinking is "about open communication, questioning, and problem-solving through inquiry and, ultimately, continuous learning" (Garrison, 2016, p. 7).

If a teacher takes on the challenge of establishing a community of inquiry in his or her classroom, here is a useful statement of seven principles of teaching practice central to the COI framework. The principles are as follows:

1. Plan for the creation of open communication and trust.
2. Plan for critical reflection and discourse.

3. Establish community and cohesion.
4. Establish inquiry dynamics.
5. Sustain respect and responsibility.
6. Sustain inquiry that moves to resolution.
7. Ensure assessment is congruent with intended process and outcomes (Garrison, 2016, p. 88).

These principles guide the design of the instruction, providing greater flexibility adapting to participants' developing needs and interests. (See Garrison [2016] for a more detailed discussion of the COI framework.)

WHAT IS MEANT BY INQUIRY?

We engage in inquiry all the time from the day we are born to this very moment. Here, however, we explore the notion of inquiry as it applies to a COI on the local level or on a more generalized level to the Great Conversation of Humankind itself. Garrison's (2016) description of inquiry is well suited to what we have in mind in the classroom COI context:

> It is a flexible transaction where existing knowledge and experience is subject to questioning, interpretation and transformation. . . . [It] transforms previous knowledge and experience and this becomes material for future inquires. . . . [It] is socially situated and dependent upon a community of inquiry. . . . Inquiry embedded in a learning community is focused on collaboratively exploring problems, constructing meaning, and validating understanding. (p. 56)

When participating in a COI, as you do when using the scripts in this course, your ability to discover your own and others' biases or misconceptions is revealed. How important it is to do that now rather than later when you are teaching or, worse, never. Through these discussions you will find that your ability to understand new information and share it with one another is amplified through continued participation in the scripted COI discussion process.

It is also likely that being cognizant of the course of inquiry in a COI will further develop your own critical thinking (Bai, 2009; Kennedy & Kennedy, 2013, as cited in Garrison, 2016). This metacognitive awareness should further sharpen your skills as a host of the thinking and learning processes central to COI classrooms experience and the Great Conversation itself.

PROFESSIONAL COMMITMENT

No one is asking you to become a teacher. Quite the contrary. In most cases you are coming before the state, your local community, or a school board and asking that you be given access to the community's most valuable resource, its children. You come before the authorities and ask for this privilege. Presumably, you are requesting this privilege because you believe you can help children and make the world a better place.

Certainly the authorities who award teaching certificates/licenses and the personnel officers who offer teaching candidates' jobs do so because they believe granting this privilege will lead to better outcomes for a number of their students. In granting this opportunity to you, authorities believe that you have properly prepared and you will now honor the heavy responsibility of caring for and bettering the next generation.

You are best able to honor that responsibility by helping students become more adept at figuring out the world within which they live. In helping students to become better at figuring things out, you prepare them for entry into the Great Conversation. By successfully bringing them into the Great Conversation, you bring them into a world of reciprocal respect for each person and for a diversity of traits. Qualities are very important in our changing world.

When you bring students into the Great Conversation, it is with the goal that they will never leave. Their lifelong participation in the Great Conversation leads to more responsible citizenship, more careful workmanship, and enhanced personal competence and confidence. Truly all this amounts to a very heavy duty indeed. But it is a duty you volunteered to undertake. Your role as a teacher is defined first and foremost by the pedagogical obligations you have undertaken.

MORAL FOUNDATIONS

Before proceeding further into teacher morality and professional ethics, it is instructive to consider what the collective sciences of biology, economics, mathematical game theory, and psychology have to say about the cognitive origins and development of human moral experience generally (Chomsky, 2016; Gintis, 2017; Sapolsky, 2017). Policies, laws, moral principles, and traditions along with respect for persons are not simply contrived out of thin air. They each exist because human thinking and instinct make them relevant to community and to professional life in particular.

Evolutionists are generally agreed that from the eusocial insects like many species of ants and termites, to pods of whales and dolphins, and to herd animals of all kinds, cooperation has emerged as an invaluable asset to those organisms (Maestripieri, 2012; Sapolsky, 2017). Among felines, for instance, the gift of amazing speed benefits jaguars and cheetahs in the hunt for prey. In contrast, the slower lions are successful because they compensate through cooperative hunting strategies. Even the prey such as zebras and wildebeests best survive on the African savannahs by staying close to the herd and not isolated to be consumed by predators.

Thirty-plus years of biological investigations have demonstrated the evolutionary value to herd animals of cooperation (Gintis, 2017; Nowak & Coakley, 2013). In addition, studies have shown that failure to cooperate within one's herd is costly both to the individual and to the herd (Nowak, 2006; Sober & Wilson, 1998). Mathematical game theorists and economists have shown that when a member of a herd defects from cooperation, that individual may benefit in the short run. But in the long run, as others copy the tendency to defect in pursuit of self-interest, the herd becomes fragile and may implode (Skyrms, 2004). But evolutionary pressures from both without and within the herd make cooperation more appealing to most than the pursuit of self-interest. Cooperation is an evolutionary ace for species that have the trait (Nowak & Highfield, 2011).

Humans cooperate more effectively than any other herd mammal. They do this in virtue of their richly textured language, which amplifies human ability to cooperate over time and vast expanses of territory (Chomsky, 2016). It may well be that the greatest invention of humans is not the wheel but the *promise*. A promise explicitly designates the amplification of cooperation. Monetary currency is a grand example of how promising networks allow humans to cooperate as can no other animal. Promises lead to tribes, cities, and nations. Promises make national treaties possible between hostile groups. Promises obligate people to one another.

Over thousands of years, humans have learned more about promising. Still now humans are learning how best and when to promise and how to enforce promising practices and either punish or shame transgressors. There is yet much to learn. But moral philosophy has evidenced the desire of humans to understand better the grounds of morality, the grounds of promising, and how to make more robust instinctual efforts to cooperate, despite deviants driven by self-interest from within the group and despite predation from without and all sorts of natural disasters. This is the source of moral experience and the sort of critical thinking it invites.

The moral awareness of human beings has led psychologists to search for the virtues some philosophers claim make humans better (Sterelny et al., 2013). Along with the search for virtues, humans have sought moral principles that, when followed, lead to better results for their respective groups. All this culminates in the laws, policies, and traditions of modern human communities from neighborhoods to states and nations and yes, even to school districts, schools, and your classroom. Moral awareness leads humans—when at our best—to think critically about what rules, customs, and policies that are put in place will likely advance a shared vision (Tuomela, 2007). Getting this right is a difficult intellectual challenge.

We should think slowly and critically if we intend to get these matters right. And, no matter how well we do this thinking, we must recognize there will be need for revision from time to time. In short, this continuous reflection is part and parcel of the Great Conversation, and COIs are employed to reinvigorate the Conversation perpetually.

As a teacher, you are duty-bound to honor the tradition of your profession. As an employee, you have another set of duties outlined in school and district policies you are to follow. As a member of civil society, you have still further restrictions and obligations you are expected to adhere to. Sometimes you will be asked to help challenge some of these duties and obligations. Sometimes you will find yourself conflicted between what seem to be contradicting duties (Wagner & Simpson, 2009). What should you do in these cases?

You should think slowly. You should think long and hard. You should think critically before casting your lot with or against one or another position at issue. You should be imaginative in your employment of critico-creative thinking. For now, you should learn how to do this type of thinking, and you will have ample opportunity to learn such thinking by participating in the spirit of COI in the scripted discussions this book provides.

THE ETHICS OF TEACHING FOR CRITICAL THINKING

As mentioned earlier, we believe that using scripts in the classroom promotes critical thinking. Several of the scripts that appear later in this book relate to issues that lead you as future or practicing teachers to think reflectively and precisely. You are sure to discover that in some cases there are not any straightforward answers to the problem at hand (Qualters, 2017).

As a teacher, you are a professional. You must abide by a set of professional ethics and the moral traditions and personal commitments that have buoyed them up over the centuries (Wagner, 1996). One must acknowledge, as Chew does (2012), that "teachers have an ethical responsibility to teach information accurately and effectively, yet they must also consider the consequences of changing a student's worldview in a way the student neither sought nor expected" (p. 113).

One way to address Chew's dictum is to teach with the Great Conversation of Humankind always in mind and with the knowledge that the local community of inquiry you are leading fosters individual *autonomy*. In the classroom COI within the Great Conversation, teachers host their students' development of critico-creative thinking, encouraging them to flesh out their assumptions while learning to respect the views of others (Jenkins, 2017).

Teachers should teach thinking across the curriculum (Minnich, 2003); but what is the role of teacher education programs in this regard? First and foremost, your teacher education preparation should extend your grasp of the ethical significance and responsibilities of your profession. Obviously, knowledge is important for the critico-creative thinking that must be employed to sort through the difficult moral and professional challenges teachers face at times.

But to think through an ethical challenge requires not only a fix on what an apt solution should look like in the end but also prompt preliminary skepticism about any imposed restrictions of behavior or apt thinking style. As noted throughout this book, the "creative" part of critico-creative thinking requires an open mind to consider novel speculations (Kerr, 1996).

While one's morality stretches across the range of personal engagement with others, in the case of teacher behavior, it is tempting to restrict attention to behavioral rules. Educators also acknowledge there are specific ethical principles professional teachers ought to adopt that refer typically to "ideals, or expectations" (Murray, Gillese, Lennon, Mercer, & Robinson, 1996, p. 57). Further, to implement policy imperatives or ideals and principles in classroom management requires teachers to be open to conceptual conflict and unrelenting when it comes to ensuring reciprocal respect among all in the COI (Chew, 2012).

A GUIDE TO THINKING THROUGH ETHICAL AND MORAL PROBLEMS

As educators, you will experience much advice that is heavy-handed or remote from the specific situations you must address moment by moment. Many of those situations are saturated through and through with moral consequence. You want to do right rather than wrong. But figuring out what is right can be challenging even for the finest of scholars sitting in their studies remote from all the pressure to act now. Fortunately, more often than not, the laws of the state and the policies of your district and school are highly reliable guides to avoiding the most conspicuous errors of wrongdoing.

Unfortunately, no organization can be so perfect that it can anticipate all eventualities and prescribe morally right action ahead in each and every case. You are no doubt familiar with the adage, "There are always exceptions to the rule." So how do you know what to do if the situation you currently face is one of those exceptions?

In today's world many people, more out of frustration than insight, settle on simplistic conclusions regarding the nature of morality. Some may say, "Everyone has their own moral truths." Unwittingly, this places Mother Theresa and Adolf Hitler on the same moral footing. Others say that your culture determines right or wrong. Unfortunately, this places the heroes of the Underground Railroad in the American South and those who rescued Jews from Nazi genocide in the alleged wrong while acknowledging the oppressors as morally righteous.

Finally, others conclude that whatever the law says is right, is right. But laws have prohibited women and minorities from voting, limited preachers from free speech from the pulpit, and prevented unpopular views from ever having an open hearing.

There is much that is troubling about each of these positions. And we are not in a position to steer you toward a litany of all the right things you ought to do in your professional life. We cannot even provide you with a criterion for recognizing close cases in which it is troublesome whether or not some policy should be followed. On the other hand, as a book dedicated to showing you more about deep thinking for guiding your professional life ahead, we do have guidelines to help you avoid being morally responsible. It is wrong to be morally irresponsible.

Moral responsibility is not about right or wrong behavior. Moral responsibility as you will shortly see is about conscientious reflection in the face of moral challenges. We cannot crank out algorithms for securing moral truth. There are guidelines, however, that can help you identify whether or not you have been responsibly conscientious when addressing a moral challenge. To focus your attention on developing moral responsibility, we make use of some relevant details from Kierstead and Wagner's (1993) *The Ethical, Legal, and Multicultural Foundations of Teaching*.

Although paying attention to each element in the elements of ethical analysis will not guarantee a morally right decision, slow thinking through each element ensures that at the very least, you tried to be thoroughly responsible.

THE ELEMENTS OF ETHICAL ANALYSIS

When an ethical problem is sufficiently difficult and time for analysis is available, every serious moral decision maker should tag, or address, each one of the following elements before drawing a final conclusion about some matter of morality:

1. Due attention must be given to each relevant argument for or against a course of action or adopting a rule or policy.

    a. This requires that moral decision makers possess a certain amount of experience and a capacity for imagination. The imaginative recall of personal experiences allows the moral agent to develop a sense of the relative range of inquiry.

b. This requires moral agents be wary of fallacious forms of reasoning. Arguments that are contradictory or in some other way unintelligible are not relevant to solving a problem.
2. Due attention must be given to all available and relevant empirical information.
   a. Decision makers must know how to identify evidence descriptive of the circumstances. This knowledge is acquired both through experience of similar cases in the past and knowledge of research studies descriptive of characteristic patterns of behavior.
   b. Decision makers must understand the limitations of their observations, as well as limitations inherent in the process of accumulating scientific data. (For example, optical illusions cause people to "see" things that do not exist. And statistical studies describe features of *groups*, not necessarily attributes of any *one member* of a group under study.)
3. Moral nomenclature must be aptly employed. Moral decision makers must be fastidious about the use of words such as "duty," "right," "good," "bad," or "responsibility." It just will not do to say that different words mean different things to different people. If this were truly the case, then public moral deliberation would be wholly uninformative and always amount to nothing more than an unintelligible set of grunts and groans.
4. Due attention must be given to the role of logical operators in moral thinking. Words such as "if . . . then," "ought," "thus," "therefore," "or not," "consequently," and "hence" must be used with precision to denote the giving of sufficient reasons for a claim, to establish necessary conditions for conclusions, to denote the compellingness of a moral imperative, and to announce various disclaimers. For example, "therefore" means sufficient reason has been given for a conclusion, and "necessary condition" indicates that something is required to complete an argument by itself doesn't determine any answers.
5. Moral intuitions are not to be ignored. This does not mean that intuitions are to be blindly followed or that someone should be listening to "little voices!!!!" It means that very deep-seated intuitions producing a visceral effect on the thinker should lead one to think through the problem again even if in the end there seems no solid reason to change direction in one's thinking. Moral intuitions do not refer to hunches about what should be done at the moment. They are only significant when deep-seated concerns, such as the importance of respect for others, seem profoundly challenged by a current line of thinking.
6. Political effectiveness and ambitions must not control agent moral reasoning. Political considerations are not wholly irrelevant to moral reasoning.

It is good to be tactful. And it is useful to rally others to a worthy cause under one's wise direction. However, if the agent's concern is to do the "right" thing rather than serve self-interest and immediate ambition, then the grounds of moral reasoning cannot be on grounds of self-interest. One way to imagine what this means in practice is to imagine what an altruistic behavior, rule, or policy would look like in all probable contexts.
7. Legal and social conventions must be reviewed to ascertain what the conventional wisdom may be in regard to the matter at hand. Too often we are arrogant. We think our way of thinking is better than those ways of thinking from times past. As far back as Aristotle in *Politics*, it was recognized that laws and social protocols reflect an evolved resiliency that ought to be studied and respected. Revolutionary change of long-standing traditions ought to be considered only after intense and sustained deliberation.
8. Professionals undertake special moral tasks that others may choose to avoid. The nature of these tasks is usually described in a code of ethics. But since a code of ethics can never be more than a sketch, the responsible professional must always look beyond the code to determine the range of moral obligations he or she has acquired in virtue of his or her standing as a professional. In other words, in addition to any rules, the true professional must always ask what the most dedicated professional would do in such a case.

Take a look at each element. Remember, to omit any element arbitrarily is to be irresponsible when attempting to think things through in morally charged contexts.

FURTHER COMMENTS ON EACH OF THE ELEMENTS

Element 1

What are the pro and con arguments for a course of action? Imagine how each stakeholder is likely to be affected by one or another decision. Remember, incompetent inferences increase the likelihood of inappropriate inferences.

Element 2

What empirical information is available to help frame the problem under consideration? Be alert to the possibility of observer error, the deliberating agent or that of statistical studies allegedly characterizing the type of problem immediately at hand.

Element 3

Use moral language skillfully. Not just any slipshod way of talking or thinking will do. Lives and human well-being often depend upon a moral agent's skillful use of moral terms. For example, the word "fair" doesn't mean treating everyone the same. Sometimes the most unfair thing to do is treat everyone the same. As Aristotle said, fairness is a matter of treating equals equally and unequals unequally.

Element 4

Logical operators are words that move about chunks of thought in our mind just as in the mind of a computer. Logical operators include such words as "if . . . then," "consequently," "therefore," "because," and so on.

Element 5

a. Moral intuitions are not to be ignored. This does not say intuitions are to be followed. This does not say hunches should drive our thinking. And, most certainly, this does not say you should listen to little voices inside your head. (Note: if you hear little voices in your head, seek help!)
b. Moral intuitions are a visceral feeling gripping one's gut when entertaining a possible decision. Moral intuitions do not tell us what is right or wrong. Moral intuitions function as a caution light. They alert us to the need to rethink every one of the eight elements again before proceeding further with a decision. In the presence of a genuine intuition, our decision needn't change in the end, but it does warrant further review at the moment.

Element 6

Most people want to get ahead in life. Most people want to avoid the effects of offending others and other social inconveniences. But this element reminds the agent, "It's NOT all about you!" Figure out what's morally right, and then figure out how to do the morally right thing skillfully without committing political suicide in the process.

Element 7

This is where the state codes of educator ethics district and building as well as relevant law come in. Before you conclude you have better ideas than those who make the laws or create your professional code of ethics, earnestly try to figure out why such mandates are there. The longer they have been in force, the more resilience they have shown.

Be careful before deciding the creators of such conventions are all wrong and that you alone or you and your circle of friends have seen the light. They may be wrong, and you may indeed be right, but be careful. Think of this as the caution not to be morally arrogant.

Element 8

Obviously, this too relies heavily on the state codes of ethics district and school policies; the law and the traditions of the profession from times of antiquity to the present come in. But this summons up thoughts about the moral architecture (Wagner & Simpson, 2009) that your professional organization has constructed for itself. This element also advises you to consider—in addition to the moral architecture of your professional organization—the moral architecture of the place of where you work.

The elements of ethical analysis, while not cranking out moral truth, do aid in making morally responsible decisions. But, you might ask, is it wrong to be morally irresponsible? The answer is an emphatic "Yes." Failure to be morally responsible is destructive from the level of friendship to group cohesiveness to national security and even species' survival.

To illustrate the meaning of this bold claim, consider this old joke: Jack and Jill are the best of friends. They are on a walk through the wilderness. Several hundred yards ahead, they spot a bear charging toward them. Jack turns to run but notices Jill has dropped to the ground and taken her boots off while pulling her Nikes out of her knapsack. Jack turns back to her and says, "Jill, we need to run, or we will never outrun that bear!" As Jill stands up, she looks at him sweetly and purrs, "We don't have to outrun that bear. I just have to outrun you." And with that, Jill bolts down the path.

Funny story. But let's unpack it a bit looking for failure of moral responsibility. First, however, think to yourself: Who would you rather have as a friend or a neighbor? Jack or Jill?

Jack turns to help make sure both try to escape the attacking bear. Jill immediately figures out how to save herself by sacrificing Jack. Without judging anyone's behavior, does it appear that there has been a failure to address the elements to ensure moral responsibility?

Look, for example, at Element 6. The element says that the well-being of all must be considered before drawing closure on a decision to a moral challenge. In the Jack and Jill story, as it is usually told, it seems to be accepted that Jill gave no consideration to Jack but only to herself. She was quick to abandon him, while he delayed out of concern for her. When it is friendships or communities of any size, the quicker and the number of defectors sabotage the resilience of the union. The more cooperation is a guiding consideration (Element 6), then, regardless of the eventual decision by various members of the community, the more likely the community is to survive as a unit.

Take a moment and imagine other moral challenges. Do not try to nail down an answer to what is right, but do consider how failure to consider each of the elements might increase the risk of destruction to a shared social unit. Morally responsible decision making matters.

SUMMING UP

Teaching is no mere job. Teaching is a profession, perhaps even a calling, that aims at helping students develop autonomy. Development of personal autonomy is what gives students the power to override personal wants and desires for good reason. There is no evidence that any other species can exercise such capacity, but humans can if properly instructed.

The proper instruction in autonomy is a function of developing critico-creative thinking in a COI. In addition, participation in a COI itself enhances and calls upon the further moral development of every participant. The goal then for teachers is to bring their students into their rightful place in the Great Conversation. The teacher role-models for students that as autonomy develops, a participant in the Great Conversation lives a commitment to truth seeking.

In this chapter, we have presented in some detail what this commitment entails. Acknowledging teacher duties to enhance critico-creative thinking skills in addition to moral awareness and responsibility are of utmost importance as you advance through your teacher preparation program.

Obviously, teachers' being capable of thinking critically is essential to teachers being able to role-model critical thinking. Teachers' acting morally is essential to teachers' role-modeling moral awareness and responsibility. Critico-creative thinking requires people to understand and explore assumptions that are the foundation of their thoughts and behaviors. Moral awareness and responsibility require that these critico-creative thinking skills, dispositions, and attitudes are mastered in the service of doing right by others. It is in a COI where students and teachers are able to evaluate the degree to which they are discovering how to think and behave critically.

Teachers must be willing and able to provide a classroom atmosphere that would be conducive to participating in the Great Conversation. Furthermore, in the midst of their day-to-day routine and stresses, teachers must believe that their efforts in this regard are worthwhile. It is this effort that gives teaching at any level genuine nobility.

Chapter 4

Education at the Crossroads

So often when policy makers, theorists, and other thinkers about education make recommendations for its improvement, they seem to begin from only one of two approaches. Either they draw attention to the lives of iconic geniuses or they employ statistical studies with near-reverence, despite the fact that statistical studies are inferentially about population characteristics. Both approaches have their place, but both can fail to give proper guidance.

From history we learn that Socrates taught Plato and Plato taught Aristotle and Aristotle taught Alexander the Great. Then there are stories that Einstein was slow to talk and a reluctant reader. Although in truth Einstein was an excellent student always competing for the top three positions in his gymnasium instruction (Pais, 1982). And the geniuses John Stuart Mill and Blaise Pascal demonstrated amazing intellectual agility from an early age. But most teachers will never have such students in their classes, and what works for the instruction of those particular geniuses may not work for others, not even other genius students.

With regard to statistics, since the days of Francis Galton, Karl Pearson, and Sir R. A. Fisher, educational researchers have measured, studied, and compared groups of individuals using statistical tools such as correlation coefficients, tests of significance, covariate analysis, and many more. These studies often provide invaluable information, and we refer to them on occasion in this book. Furthermore, such studies and knowledge of statistical tools are standard fare throughout anyone's training in pedagogy. But what can studies of *groups* tell a teacher, given his or her unique personality and skills and the unique individuals he or she is teaching at the moment?

We applaud educators who familiarize themselves with the lives of iconic geniuses. Likewise, we applaud educators who familiarize themselves with iconic teachers such as the fabled William James, Jaime Escalante, and

Marva Collins. There is much to learn from such familiarity. We also applaud educators for familiarizing themselves with statistical tools and the products of scientific investigation into learning. Still none of this can fully frame the problem of how to teach the particular child who stands in front of the teacher at a specific moment.

We do not expect to replace the utility of the pedagogically related practices mentioned earlier. Instead, we hope to focus more robustly on better thinking skills. As one of the authors (Paul Wagner) notes after many conversations about Bloom's taxonomy, taxonomies of thinking from Plato to Bloom do not fully frame the problem space of what counts as better thinking for this student here and now (Wagner, 1980).

Bloom, Englehart, Furst, Hill, and Krathwohl (1956) intended their taxonomy of cognitive objectives to have more utility for scientific purposes than say Plato's, but, as even Bloom himself acknowledged, no taxonomy can fully explain how to educate better thinkers (Wagner, 1980; see Anderson et al. [2001] for detail on the revised version of Bloom's original taxonomy for the cognitive domain, and see Wagner et al. [2017] for a discussion on the differences between the two taxonomies).

Critical thinking, reflection, and higher-level thinking each contributes to better thinking. But in the past half century, researchers have recognized a host of new skills in thinking (Brockman, 2013; Newell, Shaw, & Simon, 1958). Many of these new thinking strategies never had a name before the twentieth century. These new thinking strategies further augment the potent investigations evolving in the Great Conversation.

In this book, we will alert you to the existence of some of these new strategies, but our focus will be on the dialogical form of critical review and thinking. The reason for this focus is twofold. First, dialogical strategies are immediately useful in every context. They center on the question, "How do you know?"

The second reason for focusing on dialogical strategies is that in the end the utility of every other thinking strategy must be subjected to review and critical analysis by dialogical strategies (Paul, 1993). Coupled with the question, "What do you mean by the term ___?" dialogical strategies unveil for critical thinkers the eventual utility of every new thinking technology and tactic. Dialogical strategies focus always on justification and never on mere guesses or illusory solutions.

Before proceeding any further, and before introducing some of the new thinking strategies currently in development, consider the life of Ed Thorp, a living exemplar of a thinker for all seasons. Thorp is no relation to the great Native American athlete of the twentieth century, Jim Thorpe, but he does have a minority background, including immediate relatives of Filipino, Latino, and German descent. Thorp went to the second-lowest rated school in the Los Angeles school district, and he came from a poor family and a broken home. Today he might be labeled as an "at risk" student because of those factors, and his life illustrates that "at risk" does not mean "destined for failure."

Thorp grew up in a state of continual mischief, taking things apart and sometimes blowing things up, but he learned a lot about science in the process and as a result went to college on a scholarship. He advanced to a PhD program in physics, but, in order to get answers to the questions that really attracted him, he needed to pursue pure mathematics. After getting a degree in pure mathematics, he published considerable work in prestigious mathematical journals.

However, Thorp was not satisfied with achievements in formalistic reasoning, and he always engaged in dialogical reasoning as well (Thorp, 2017). For example, he asked how people know that the casinos in Nevada cannot be beaten by a card counter system. His response was to devise a system that did beat the casinos. At MIT he met up with Claude Shannon, the father of information theory, and convinced him to work together to beat the roulette wheel system. The project was again a success.

Thorp moved into university administration because he was good with people. He then made millions of dollars by developing systems for investing in the stock market. After he created his own successful hedge fund companies, he eventually began thinking about questions of economic benefit for all and questions of general morality.

In short, the point of this brief narrative is that Thorp used mathematical proof strategies, created computer algorithms, used game theoretic strategies, and constantly excelled in asking foundational "How do you know?" questions and "What do you mean by ___?" questions at every opportunity throughout life (Thorp, 2017). Thorp is a master of the law of figuring things out in the broadest array of contexts.

Thorp's skills of critical thinking, mathematical analysis, and dialogic reasoning allowed him to master and apply other thinking strategies to a broad array of life interests and theoretical and applied challenges. For example, Thorp was a major player in identifying corruption on Wall Street, and he became a public intellectual in matters of social and political theory and even morality. Thorp entered the Great Conversation early on and has role-modeled a commitment to lifelong learning and engagement in the Great Conversation of Humankind ever since.

A central moral of this story is that a robust array of better thinking skills, as Ed Thorp exhibited, must surely be an appropriate generalized direction for the education of all students. In contrast, recognition and speed of information retrieval are narrowly conceived goals for education, goals without generalized direction. So the aim for immediate performance on recognition tests sacrifices the more general goal of equipping each graduate for life in an unpredictable and often fragile world (Taleb, 2014).

As earlier chapters make clear, education in America is at an unprecedented crossroads. Mathematician Cathy O'Neil (2016) describes what happened in Washington, D.C., public schools after Mayor Adrian Fenty brought in reformer Michelle Rhee to initiate a system of accountability. Rhee, who later became superintendent, and her team, including a high-powered set of consultants, developed an assessment tool called IMPACT. The algorithm they employed used about a dozen markers to aggregate a quantitative score allegedly identifying a teacher's success.

Predictably, the algorithm overemphasized some measurements and underutilized other important measurements. To make matters worse, the algorithm did not adapt to changing contingencies. According to O'Neil (2016), the algorithm left out much information that in a world of big data could have been captured and aggregated. Moreover, the algorithm failed to acknowledge information relevant to evaluating teachers that cannot be easily quantified and aggregated. The result was that good teachers were fired, only to be rehired in some cases in more prestigious and lucrative districts.

O'Neil's (2016) thesis is that the mismanagement of mathematical models creates an environment of suspicion and intimidation. When educators have models imposed on them that they do not understand and that are used for purposes of evaluation, it is natural for them to become suspicious. As O'Neil explains, it turns out that supervisors using overly complex models have little understanding of the function of evaluation or the purpose at hand. Scores are announced and decisions imposed. Winners cheered and then worried about the next round of evaluation. Losers felt victimized because no one could clearly explain grounds for the efficacy of the model or the decisions affecting their lives.

This misuse of evaluation was exposed years ago by total quality management guru, W. Edwards Deming. Deming insisted personnel evaluation should utilize few numbers, and fear should be eliminated from the process (Deming, 2013).

Whether or not O'Neil is right in her disparagement of big data algorithms used in educational evaluation, she is certainly not alone in her lament. In the book *The Math Myth*, Andrew Hacker (2016) disparages the use of big data to inflate needs for STEM specialization. Both O'Neil and Hacker point out that data, no matter how big, can never "speak for itself." Data must always be interpreted, and interpretations always have a degree of subjectivity built into them (Arbesman, 2016; Johnson & Gluck, 2016).

Whether both of these authors are right or wrong in their criticisms of public education, the fact remains that education is at a crossroads unlike any before seen in educational policy-making. Because of twenty-first-century demands, education has been urged to produce more quantitatively and technologically skilled graduates to feed a demanding high-tech economy (Slavin, 2015).

Others demand greater accountability in the quantity and demonstrable retrieval speed of students for recollecting high-quality information (Hirsch, 2016). And there are yet more demands from other sectors of society.

Politicians, psychologists, and philosophers argue for the need to develop character in students (Lickona, 1996). Sociologists, multiculturalists, and globalists want greater focus on transcultural learning (Kierstead & Wagner, 1993). Humanists and artists fear the denigration of the sensitizing disciplines (Madsbjerg, 2017).

Because of the increased interest in health matters, such as obesity in youth, health advocates worry about the need for more exercise, better nutrition information, and further instruction in proactive health regimens (e.g., Centers for Disease Control and Prevention, 2017). And nearly everyone is concerned about bullying of all sorts in schools (Graham, 2014). Certainly, there are ways of doing more to appease the desires of each of these stakeholder groups, but there is no way to do everything for all.

After reviewing the litany of all those various groups, thinking should constitute the content and practice of education, but one glaring omission stands out. Each reformer is clear why students should know more about what that reformer wants students to know, but few have articulated a theory about what education should be. For example, theorists from Aristotle to John Dewey, R. S. Peters, Paul Hirst, and Israel Scheffler have always been willing to tackle the big questions about educational purpose (Aristotle, 2009; Dewey, 1916; Hirst, 1975; Peters, 1966; Scheffler, 1990).

There are decisions to be made. The public schools cannot be all things to all people. In fact, public schools focus on teaching skills to middle-class populations (Lindgren & Suter, 1985). Moreover, it is not clear that schools should try to be what most people want in their schools. The great Spanish intellectual Ortega y Gasset (1985) warned long ago that the masses ignore the advice of experts at their own peril. Maybe so, but these days it is not clear who the experts are. Even if we could identify the relevant experts, it is not clear that they would agree on much at the moment. In addition to intellectual turmoil among policy makers, "fake news" and the Internet drive further confusion among the public-at-large about a number of things affecting education (Ladson-Billings, 2016).

Education is not a manufacturing problem. Neither an algorithm nor the assembly line can deliver what the nation's students need to thrive and contribute to their communities (Manley & Hawkins, 2010). Necessary change will come about when deep-thinking teachers speak out loud and clear to a public that is increasingly desperate for improvement in educational practices.

Through these chapters and the scripts ahead, teachers are invited to think deeply about what they are preparing to do. When all is said and done, it is the classroom teacher who makes any approach to student learning a success

(Shermis & DiVesta, 2011). It is time articulate teachers step forward and explain to the public the real needs of classroom instruction aimed at preparing students for a lifetime of participation in the Great Conversation.

Surely there are few who would dissent from the claim that, at the very least, education should aim at a better life for all who participate. Note the key word, "participate." Going to school is not the same as participation in education. Ideally, students are brought to school so that teachers who know how to model participation in the Great Conversation can do so, and, in the process, they initiate students into a lifetime of participation with one another in that Conversation.

Social scientists and philosophers will always work at determining the details of what a better life should be. At this point it is enough for the reader to settle for the modest prescription that education should, at the very least, increase students' skills at figuring out the world around them (Siegel, 2017). Unless one lives inside a computer, the world the students will face will not be a giant multiple-choice test. The world that will challenge them, as it does us all, is fluid and inexhaustible in possibilities (Deutsch, 2012).

Consequently, at every level, education (as opposed to training) should be about helping people *figure out* some aspect of the world. Hence, the repeated references to the law of figuring things out (LFTO).

The LFTO states that, despite anything a person has learned, he or she must figure out what to say or do at the moment in apprehension of some action (Searle, 2001). The LFTO requires drawing on all appropriate cognitive resources and protocols (and maybe even creating new ones) to direct further attention and plan a course of action. No education, no training, and no schooling process can substitute for this engagement between intellect and worldly reality (Sloman & Fernbach, 2017).

This book and the scripted discussions toward the end are intended to induce responsible teachers into the process of figuring out their professional destiny as both guardians and instigators of good thinking. These teachers must then be capable of serving as hosts of that Conversation. The Great Conversation is about addressing big questions, open-mindedness, rigor of reflection, respect for fellow participants, and more (Wagner et al., 2016, 2017). Engagement in the Great Conversation, as it centers on education itself, leads participating teachers to share in an appropriate search for professional destiny.

In this instance of the Great Conversation, preservice teachers and practicing teachers figure out the world that challenges and surrounds them in their respective nations and its schools. This is not a book of algorithms for teaching practice. Neither is it a compliance manual for accommodating state or national directives to teachers. And finally, the book does not prescribe a grab bag of tricks alleged to be motivation attention getters with appropriate reinforcements. Instead, the goal of this book is far more practical than any of these commonplace distractors in contemporary education.

In this Great Conversation teachers come to realize that not only have the nation's schools come to a crossroads in matters of proportional funding of programs, curricula, technologically dependent strategies, and so on, but also a crossroads is what one always finds when responsibly investigating big questions. Policy makers have brought national attention to the crossroads in education and to the need to make education itself, a part of the Great Conversation (Wagner & Simpson, 2009). Teachers must take a leading role in the Great Conversation as it pertains to education and explain some of the subtleties that make creating a truly comprehensive theory, plan, and set of protocols difficult to conceive.

The crossroads of education in the Great Conversation begins with readers here and now. Think deeply about this or any other subject, and discover what it means to engage in the dialogic of philosophy. Whenever someone thinks deeply about any subject, the person finds him or herself, sooner or later, doing philosophy (Paul, 1993; Wagner, 1986). Whenever a person asks "How do you know?" and when the offered justification for a claim is substantial, that person is engaging others in philosophy. The dialogic of philosophy is encountered when the resources of the sciences and humanities have been pushed to current limits.

Drawing on all the reader has learned in a variety of courses dealing with the sciences of pedagogy, attention must now turn toward using this information according to the LFTO. The resources of various knowledge silos must be brought to the fore to ferret out means for creating a dialogic community of inquiry in every classroom. In the end, education should lead not to speed and range of recognition but rather to serious reflection leading from knowledge silo to crossroads and from crossroads back to increasingly robust knowledge silos for human meaning and flourishing. At the crossroads there will always be both new doubts and new insights (Deutsch, 2012).

Doubt is what rescues thinkers from intellectual complacency. Doubt brings reflective teachers to the crossroads of educational purpose, policy, and practice. Doubt hosts application of the LFTO. When doubt is lost and certainty enters in, there is no motivation to figure anything out. Before continuing, some further attention to components of the LFTO must be mentioned.

CRITICO-CREATIVE THINKING

Critico-creative thinking is the oldest and the most generalizable component of the LFTO. For a long time, people have been trying to figure out how best to figure things out. Aristotle, for example, conjured rules of logic which, when used to monitor hypotheses and speculations, revealed whether or not conclusions reached seemed to hold tight, given the assumptions with which thinkers began.

In addition, Aristotle and other thinkers of Greek antiquity recognized that exactness of shared speech is essential to successful evaluation and shared hypothesizing. So the master questions of "How do you know" and "What do you mean by the term___?" are of ancient heritage. They continue to command central stage in the Conversation today (Dwyer, 2017).

Unfortunately, the term "critical thinking" has on occasion been associated with closed-mindedness, mean-spiritedness, and bias (Willingham, 2007). As Daniel Levitin (2016) laments in response to such judgments, "Critical thinking doesn't mean we disparage everything: it means that we try to distinguish between claims with evidence and those without" (p. xxi). However, the reasons for these associations are understandable.

In the first case, for example, some have attempted to quash others' speculations by dismissing them as "mere speculation." The second misguided criticism of critical thinking is that it is mean-spirited. People may indeed be mean-spirited at times, but that has nothing inherently to do with the process of creating sound arguments or evaluating the possible soundness of arguments. Stephen J. Gould, the youngest person ever to become a full professor at Harvard University, was well known for his razor-sharp criticism of flimsy arguments, but he was also generous and kind to earnest learners. Neither sound arguments nor critical reviews of proposed justifications necessitate an attitude of mean-spiritedness on anyone's part.

In short, mean-spirited people can be found anywhere and in any context. Still, it is important to recognize that mean-spiritedness is not a necessary part of argument construction, evaluation, or dialogical reasoning in general. In fact, mean-spiritedness is also antithetical to participation in the Great Conversation because it betrays a lack of respect for the participants. Hence, it is unacceptable in any learning environment notable for an emphasis on critical thinking and shared participation in the Great Conversation.

Bias may be unintentional, but a function of critical thinking is to draw attention to distractions caused by bias infecting sound reasoning. Of course, intentional bias is deadly to critical thinking, and, finally, reckless thinking ignores the perils of being biased and is nearly as destructive to planning and truth-seeking as intentional bias.

It is easy to imagine people who applaud themselves as "critical thinkers." It is also easy to imagine such people belittling the reasoning of religious people, rural people, scientists, political activists, wealthy people, poor people, ethnicities, and many others, not for demonstrable errors of reasoning but rather for endorsing alleged "wrong" reasons in the first place! The trouble with such denouncing of others' thinking is that reasons cannot be designated as wrong in the absence of some substantive, critical review.

Everyone has a right to his/her own opinions. But, when people denounce the thoughtful arguments others earnestly set forth, they silence dialogic practice and they poison the atmosphere of respect necessary in a community of inquiry. The truth-claims of earnest participants in the Great Conversation deserve to have their justifications for such claims reviewed respectfully and substantively. This is the dialogical reasoning that licenses plausible claims, plans of action, and even the worthiness of other thinking strategies.

Teachers have a professional and moral duty to role-model critical thinking (Wagner et al., 2016). In part, this means they must never disparage another person's claim or argument simply because they do not like it. Teachers must also encourage an atmosphere in the classroom wherein earnest challenge of the teacher or the required curriculum's truth claims is always open to critical review—again, by earnest inquirers. Teachers who do not role-model earnest inquiry or deny students the opportunity to engage in earnest inquiry are unable to host episodes of the Great Conversation and should not be in the classroom.

Unfortunately, because of misguided practices resulting in close-mindedness, mean-spiritedness, and bias in contexts where people claim to be critically thinking, critical thinking has sometimes been confused with simply being critical. This is a horribly destructive consequence in classrooms where excellence in inquiry should always be paramount.

Critical thinking is single-minded truth-seeking. Critical thinking is not rumor mongering, gossip, reckless opinion-making, hostile criticism, or anything else of similar ilk. To avoid at least some misguided interpretations associated with critical thinking, some advocates began using the hyphenated term "critico-creative thinking." In critico-creative thinking, there is encouragement for thinkers to speculate, to entertain wonderment, and so on (Kuhn, 1999).

The Philosophy for Children movement (P4C) is a paradigm of how critico-creative thinking may be brought into the classroom. Advocates of P4C begin with creating an atmosphere of shared wonder and then proceed to prompt speculative hypotheses to be shared and subjected to review by others in the community of inquiry (Lipman, 2003). This approach has been shown to be very effective when managed by those who understand philosophical reflection and how to manage students in a community of inquiry (Fair et al., 2015a, 2015b; Maiorana, 2016; Topping & Trickey, 2007a, 2007b). Understanding philosophical reflection is tantamount to critico-creative thinking. To be effective, teachers must be sincere and skilled truth-seekers themselves.

No one can role-model what they themselves have not developed. Teachers who excel at critico-creative thinking role-model rather than teach the skills and dispositions. Students learn the skills and dispositions not by being taught but by being immersed in the practice of such engagements with others—particularly their teachers (Wagner et al., 2017). Teachers who role-model critico-creative thinking have discovered that over time, such thinking instincts have become second nature to them—it is not a canned performance to be measured by behavioral objectives. To sum it up, skills and dispositions are caught, not taught (Hirst, 1975; Peters, 1966).

There is more to satisfying the LFTO than people getting "right" answers. In fact, the LFTO is more potent in its detection and removal of wrong answers than in the divination of right answers. This is why critico-creative thinking is central to the LFTO but not exhaustive of it. The LFTO also draws upon everything of value in the critical thinking movement and adds cutting-edge novel cognitive tactics evolving in the various sciences. The LFTO sets the highest bar. It is intended to be exhaustive of thinking excellence. The LFTO encourages thinkers to employ various and potent strategies for moving away from error in any contemplated action or search for truth. Now, it is time to take a look at some of these strategies.

Chapter 5

Critico-Creative Thinking

Tools and Strategies

LOGIC: FORMAL AND INFORMAL

Doubt is what rescues us from intellectual complacency. From the time of antiquity, scholars have sought formal systems for minimizing unavoidable doubt and ensuring the truth of conclusions (Kvanvig, 2014). Aristotle is one who is known for developing logic to demonstrate the iron-clad reasoning behind a deductive (truth-guaranteeing) argument. Pythagoras, another teacher from classical antiquity, created proofs in geometry. For example, the Pythagorean theorem was intended to provide iron-clad justification for his claim about the square of the hypotenuse of right triangles being equal to the sum of the squares of the other two sides.

Fast-forward more than a thousand years and you find logicians such as Thomas Aquinas, Peter Abelard, William of Ockham, and others pressing forward the use of formal logic to establish truths about the heavens, a creator, and our final destinies. Still later, in the nineteenth and twentieth centuries, there were dramatic strides to further develop formal logic (Misak, 2016).

Much of the early success in computer programming owed much to these efforts. Pick up any textbook in formal logic in college mathematics or philosophy course, and you will see what this is all about (e.g., Copi & Cohen, 2008). Indeed, all of Claude Shannon's work in information theory began when he first encountered these logicians in a college philosophy course while he was studying to become an electrical engineer (Soni & Goodman, 2017).

To see why formal logic might matter, consider the process used to test hypotheses. Suppose Tom goes to the doctor because he is feeling bad. The doctor formulates a diagnostic hypothesis (H) that Tom has malaria. The doctor reasons that *if* her hypothesis H about malaria is correct, *then* that would imply the prediction (P) that Tom should have a pattern of recurrent fevers. Then she obtains records of Tom's temperature, and presumably either the pattern of recurrent fever is in the temperature data or it is not. So the situation can be represented as either the prediction does not come true or the prediction does come true:

1. If H, then P   4. If H, then P
2. P is false   5. P is true
3. H is false   6. H is true

Look carefully at these two patterns because there is a distinction in logical power between them. On the left, *if* the implication about a recurrent fever pattern is correct and *if* the temperature data really do not match the prediction, *then* the hypothesis that Tom has malaria *cannot* be correct. In contrast, on the right side, even if the prediction about recurrent fevers is correctly inferred from the hypothesis and even if the temperature data do in fact indicate recurrent fevers, there is *no guarantee* that the hypothesis that Tom has malaria is correct. The reason there is no guarantee is, of course, that lots of things besides malaria can cause fevers.

People have drawn a couple of morals from this bit of formal logic. One is that a hypothesis that does not make any predictions about what can be observed cannot be tested. A second moral is that negative or falsifying results have much more logical strength than positive or verifying results. When a prediction from a hypothesis we are testing fails to come true and we are satisfied that all of the conditions for a legitimate test were in place, then no matter how appealing or obviously true the hypothesis *seemed to be*, it cannot be true. We must abandon the hypothesis and move on to a new idea.

Beyond formal logic, logicians from Aristotle onward quickly recognized that their tools of formal logic did not cover all that matters to good thinking (Misak, 2016). Learning not to draw conclusions based upon what everyone else says (the fallacious appeal to popularity), relying too much on authority (illegitimate appeal to authority), recklessly imagining a cascade of events following from one simple act or suspicion (slippery slope fallacy) are all examples of fallacies, that is, errors in effective thinking.

Fallacies are common, and this is why experts in thinking take notice of them (e.g., Wagner et al., 2017; appendix C). There is no theory of fallacy. The best that can be done is to catalog them under the rubric: informal logic. Acquaintance with informal logic can be quite useful to teachers, for instance, when teaching students to write essays with arguments to support a thesis.

Informal logic records standard fallacies in our thinking. Typically, these fallacies are detected through the Great Conversation's central questions "How do you know?" and "What do you mean by the term ____?" In general, the more one knows about informal fallacies the more ability a person has to construct arguments of his or her own and to recognize the ill-constructed arguments of others. Informal logic can be thought of as part of the mental hygiene of the Great Conversation.

There are many textbooks on informal logic (e.g., Ennis, 1969). The reader might find all he or she needs to start by reviewing Appendix C in *Focus on Thinking* (Wagner et al., 2017). Teachers, who themselves have learned something about informal logic, will delight in their students acquiring skills of critical evaluation, more meticulous reading of an assignment (Beers & Probst, 2017), and more careful articulation of positions they wish to defend.

PROBABILISTIC CONSTRUCTIONS AND STATISTICAL EVALUATIONS

Departing from these traditional divisions of logic, much expertise in probabilistic thinking has developed in the past 400 years. Beginning with people such as the Bernoulli family members, Blaise Pascal, and Thomas Bayes, potent applications of probabilistic thinking exploded in popularity in the late nineteenth and early twentieth centuries. First, in the skillful hands of Francis Galton and, then, in the hands of statisticians such as Ronald Fisher and Karl Pearson, probabilistic thinking rose to extraordinary prominence (Sukel, 2016).

Finally, in the past fifty years, expertise in probabilistic thinking has become more specialized. For examples, see review journals such as the *Educational Researcher* and *Educational Statistics* (Langford, 2016). In addition, statistical assessments now routinely guide decision making in biomedicine, high-energy physics, pharmacology, product quality analysis, political analysis, marketing evaluation, and risk analysis (Peterson, 2017). Those interested in teaching critical thinking need to know as much about these matters as they can learn, both in order to evaluate educational research and to role-model statistical inquiry and evaluation for students (Wagner, 2006).

There are two areas of inductive reasoning where every participant in the Great Conversation should have a grasp of some of their basic principles. The first is generalizing on the basis of a sample. We have no choice but to generalize to cope with the world as we experience it. But the generalizations we make can be more firmly founded depending on the samples that underlie them. The issue is how representative our samples are likely to be. Representativeness rests on two considerations: (1) sample size and (2) sample collection process.

This is an instance where most generalize on the basis of a sample, often without paying much attention to what they are doing. We generalize about people we encounter. We attribute to them characteristics we suppose are accurate representations of the sort of people they are. We describe people as patient or impatient, honest or dishonest, punctual or not punctual, and sometimes going through a whole catalogue of human virtues and failings. We often make these judgments of character on very little evidence. Sometimes it is on the basis of a single encounter!

Moreover, seldom, with some exceptions, do we encounter people in a wide variety of situations where we can gauge their behavior. Teachers typically encounter students in a school setting but less often at play in their neighborhoods, in their churches, or on a job. Accordingly, often the samples of student behavior that form the basis of teachers' judgments about the students are severely limited in their variety.

Those samples are likely to over- or underrepresent certain types of behavior. This makes them biased samples. Bias in this sense is not about prejudicial thoughts but about flaws built into the sampling process. These flaws make the sample less representative of the proffered generalization. So our conclusions about people are often based on samples that are very small and/or biased, and we should be aware of these limitations so that we are not overconfident in making those judgments.

The second area that everyone should know something about is the design of experiments. We experiment to gather evidence that will allow us to figure out cause-and-effect linkages in a complex world. The "gold standard" for this endeavor is the randomized controlled clinical trial (RCT). Although there are many complications that need to be dealt with in actual cases, the fundamental idea is straightforward. If a drug company claims they have developed a new flu vaccine, they need to give evidence that it works and that it is relatively safe. They cannot just give the vaccine to a group of twenty people and note that, after flu season has passed, only six of them got the flu. That could just be a fluke due to chance.

What needs to happen is something more like this scenario. The drug company recruits 400 test subjects and then randomly splits them into groups of 200 each, the control group and the experimental group, which receives the new vaccine. The point, of course, is to see whether there is a difference between the two groups in the rate at which they get the flu. The groups need to be as much alike as possible in every factor that relates to their chances of getting the flu. This means that the drug company needs to assure us that they "controlled for" all of the factors that could cause a difference in the infection rate between the two groups.

If we are convinced that the drug company did succeed in controlling for the influence of all of the other factors, then, if there is a difference between the two groups, there is a chance that the difference is due to the new flu vaccine. But this is only a chance. If the difference is very small, say 52 out of

200 infected in the experimental group versus 54 out of 200 infected in the control group, then it is quite possible the small difference is due to random factors. But if it is a larger difference, like 52 infected in the experimental group versus 84 infected in the control group, then the drug company can say this is a "statistically significant difference," a difference that is, in this context, unlikely to be due to random factors.

The point is that when people say that "studies show" that something works, whether that something is a new vaccine or a new way of teaching arithmetic, it matters whether those studies involve credible RCTs. Over the years, all sorts of interventions and procedures in the fields of medicine and education have been touted as the next great thing. Too often there is at best only a slender base of evidence that these interventions and procedures actually work as claimed.

Of course, in school settings we cannot always conduct a RCT. Another strategy that can be employed to gather evidence to help figure out what works and what does not is action research. Please consult appendix B on action research in order to find out more about it and how to do it.

DECISION THEORY

Experts offer training in statistical thinking, inductive thinking, and analytical thinking to further the potency of an individual's critical thinking skills, (e.g., Bermudez, 2009) and to give each of us strategies for making better decisions under conditions of uncertainty. Conditions are uncertain when it appears there is no way to gather all relevant evidence from which a truth-guaranteeing deduction can be made. These strategies advance thinking beyond mere guessing or relying on intuitions (Cuypers & Martin, 2013).

Sometimes, admittedly, intuitions must be relied upon (Gigerenzer, 2015), and intuitions sometimes contain more insight than is apparent on the surface. In addition, most decisions people make throughout the day require what Daniel Kahneman (2013) calls "fast thinking." Fast thinking is what animates deliberate action at a particular moment. Fast thinking makes up most of our daily decision making.

When better thinking is called for, however, as in the context of the Great Conversation, Kahneman says we should utilize "slow thinking" strategies. In contrast to fast thinking, slow thinking acknowledges the enormity of an impending intellectual challenge and settles in to think it through. Blaise Pascal is generally recognized as the father of decision making under uncertainty (Gigerenzer, 2002). Pascal had an atheist friend who was a gambler. His friend said there is no way *to know* whether or not there is eternal reward or punishment; so why should anyone behave as some religion might dictate?

Pascal agreed that there was no way of knowing such a thing (Pascal, 1671/1995). But, if the possible reward is *infinite*, eternal bliss, then, even if there is only a meager chance of obtaining it, Pascal argued that it is a smarter bet to behave in accord with the religious injunctions rather than simply going for the *finite* reward of "grabbing for all gusto" one can in this world. This is called Pascal's wager (Rescher, 1985), and, whether Pascal's wager is ultimately sound or not, it is an example of decision making under conditions of uncertainty. It demands slow thinking to fulfill the requirements of the LFTO.

Benjamin Franklin was something of a forerunner of decision theory (Christian & Griffiths, 2016). He once counseled a friend, who was deliberating about whether or not to marry, to make up a list of traits that he valued or disvalued about a young lady. He further advised his friend to add weighted quantitative value to the pluses and minuses utilizing some simple scale, say 1–5. Afterward, Franklin advised, just sum the results. A positive result indicates the friend should marry the lady. A negative sum says he should not marry her (Christian & Griffiths, 2016). This is a clean system for aggregating data. Do you think this aggregating of data is sufficient for securing accurate answers in such contexts?

Franklin was not the only famous person to advise making lists of positive and negative traits to settle affairs of the heart. Charles Darwin famously did the same when he was considering whether or not to marry his cousin, Lady Wedgwood. While such list-making by intellectual luminaries for the purposes of marriage may bring a chuckle to mind, is it not common today for people to make up lists for evaluating the "right" spousal candidates?

In recent years, economists, business decision theorists, and applied mathematicians have joined together with some psychologists and philosophers to develop robust and rigorously detailed protocols for managing decisions. Such decisions can range across conclusions regarding prudently drawn classroom management strategies (Wagner, 2010), marketing schemes, personnel policies, and logistics to name but a few. In general, decision theory involves data mining, the design of algorithms, and the creation of branching "decision trees" for breaking a decision protocol into the relevant steps. Decision theory is a slow-thinking generalized strategy in both theory and application.

Today the ground floor of decision theory is the construction of decision trees. It will take but a moment to explain the general idea behind decision trees. This too is a slow-thinking strategic tool, and higher-level thinkers can exploit it to lay out a justification for a course of action in more technical contexts.

Assembling the material for a decision tree starts with determining that a particular situation calls for a decision. Next, we need to determine what are the options in that situation, that is, what are the different actions that we can actually take. Then for each action, we need to consider what are the possible outcomes, both positive and negative. To complete the analysis, each outcome must be assigned a value using a common standard (often this is a monetary value in corporate decision making), and finally we must say what we think the probability is of each of the outcomes.

Of course, at each of these steps, something can go wrong. It may be that we think we have a choice of how to respond in a situation when we really do not. (Keep in mind, however, that a choice to stand pat and do nothing in a situation is still a choice.) Or we can overlook choices that are actually open to us. One common mistake in this connection is to lay out a number of different actions to be chosen and then to *assume without thinking about it* that we can choose only one thing to do from the list when maybe we can do more than one thing. And, if we can overlook choices, how much easier is it to overlook possible outcomes? In fact, much has been made of the "law of unintended consequences," which urges us to consider that, all too often, we do not know the full range of consequences, both positive and negative, of our choices.

However, even if we bear these cautions in mind, the strategy of constructing a decision tree forces us to be up front and explicit about each of the aspects of the decision situation: the actions to be chosen, the outcomes that are possible, the values of the outcomes, and their probabilities. Making these things explicit gives the decision maker a chance to reflectively challenge his or her thought processes and raise appropriate questions. Also, in many situations (and this is no small benefit), thinking through the decision in this way enables one to explain to others exactly why the decision seemed at the time to be a reasonable and responsible one.

Here is an example that lays out the basics of this approach. Consider Sam who is trying to decide what to do on a Saturday night. Sam has reduced his choices to just two: go to a movie or stay home and watch TV. In thinking about the movie option, Sam estimates that he has a 70% chance of having a really good time, an experience he rates as a +8 on his rating scale that ranges from a +10 for the very best experience to a −10 for an absolute disaster. But he allows that there is a 30% chance that he will find the movie to be an irritating bad time for a −4. For the stay and watch TV option, Sam estimates that he has an 80% chance of having a moderately good time, a +5 on his rating scale, and a 20% chance of being bored for the evening, a −2.

We will put this information into a decision tree, and there are a number of conventions for drawing decision trees. We will use one of the common ones here, where a rectangle represents the decision situation, ovals connected by lines to the rectangle indicate our choices of possible actions, and triangles connected by lines to the circles indicate possible outcomes of those choices. The probability of the outcome can be a number on the line leading from the circle to that outcome and the value of the outcome as assessed by the decision maker can be contained in the triangle. Here is what Sam's decision tree would look like (see figure 5.1).

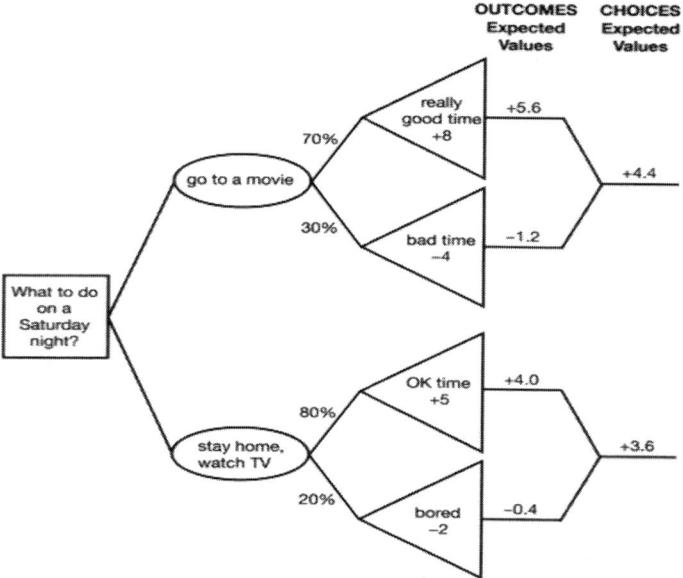

Figure 5.1. Decision Tree No. 1 Sam's Decision

One more thing is needed. We need a *decision rule* that will tell us how to use all of this information to make a decision. A very commonly used decision rule is *to make the choice that maximizes expected value*. The concept of expected value combines the value of each possible outcome with its probability. The decision maker computes the expected value of each outcome by multiplying the value of the outcome by its probability. Then the decision maker adds up all of the expected values for the outcomes of a given choice, and the result is the expected value for that choice. Use a similar process for each choice, and at the end you should be able to compare the expected value of each choice to the expected value of the others.

In Sam's case, the movie option has one outcome valued at +8 that is 70% likely, so 8 × .7 = +5.6 expected value for that outcome. But the expected value for the negative outcome rated as a −4 and 30% possible is the product of −4 × .3 = −1.2. When the −1.2 is added to +5.6, the result is +4.4 for the expected value of that choice.

The stay-at-home choice has one moderately OK outcome rated at +5 that is 80% likely, so +5 × .8 equals +4.0, whereas the boredom possible outcome of the choice is rated as −2 and 20% likely, so its expected value is −2 × .2, which equals −0.4. That makes the total expected value for the stay-at-home choice +4.0 + −0.4, which is +3.6. So, clearly, if these calculations are correct and if the rule is to make the choice that maximizes expected value, then Sam will decide to go to the movies since the expected value of the movie choice is +4.4, which is greater than the +3.6 expected value of the stay-at-home choice.

Here is a second example that is inspired by a real situation and involves a case of medical decision making (see Figure 5.2). Suppose Bob is seventy years old and has a heart attack. Very fortunately for Bob, he is playing golf with his doctor at the time and the golf course is only five minutes from the hospital. After a few days of recovery and diagnostic work, Bob is faced with a situation that requires a choice of how to go forward. The doctor tells Bob that there are fundamentally only two choices, to undergo open-heart surgery or simply to take medication.

Furthermore, Bob is told that the surgery has a 90% chance of restoring him to a fully functioning active lifestyle, but there is a 10% chance that he will die on the operating table. With the choice of taking medication, the chance of a full recovery is about 1%, and there is a 99% chance of going on living but at a noticeably reduced level of activity. Bob was a fighter pilot in World War II, and, not surprisingly, he elects to have the surgery, and the story ends happily with the surgery being successful.

But if this decision were to be laid out in a decision tree, we would have to make explicit the values Bob is assigning to the possible outcomes. Let us say that Bob gives a +10, the top rating on his scale, for the surgery's possible outcome of complete recovery to full functioning, and he gives a −10, the worst possible rating, for dying on the table. For the medication option, the value of the complete recovery outcome for Bob is again a +10, but Bob really does not like the prospect of living with reduced activity, and he rates it as a −8.

With these ratings, the expected value of the surgery option is the sum of the expected value of the good outcome, which is +10 × .9 for a +9, and the expected value of bad outcome, which is −10 × .1 for a −1. So, the expected value of the surgery option is the sum of +9 + −1 for a +8. For the medication option, the good outcome figures are +10 × .01, which equals +.1, while the bad outcome is −8 × .99 for −7.92. The total expected value for the medication option is then the sum of +.1 + −7.92, which equals −7.82. If Bob is following the rule of making the choice that maximizes expected value, then he should choose surgery since a +8 is much greater than a −7.82.

Obviously, there might be different choices made if (1) other options were open, (2) the probabilities assigned to the outcomes differed—for example, what if the surgery was riskier—and especially (3) a different decision maker applied different values to the outcomes. But there is one more thing to consider: What if the decision maker employs a different decision rule? In this

64   Chapter 5

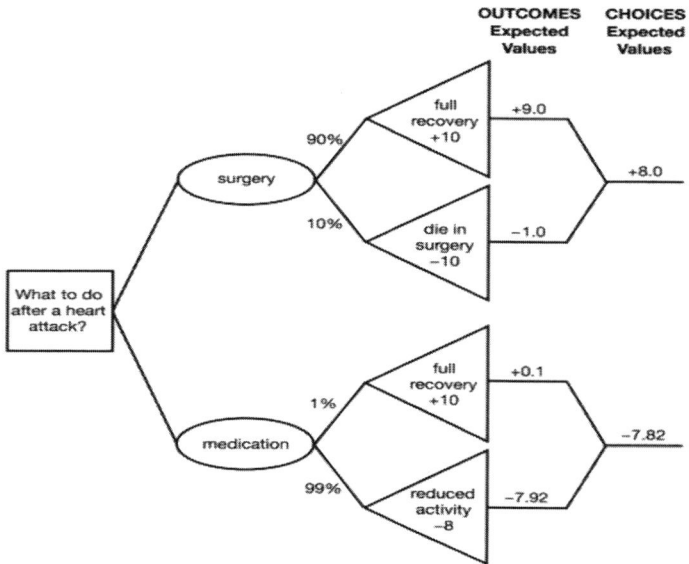

Figure 5.2.   Decision Tree No. 2 Bob's Decision

particular case, for example, one thing the medication choice has going for it is that it avoids the worst possible outcome, dying on the operating table. If someone is averse to taking big risks, then he or she may follow the rule of picking the option that has the least bad outcome, which in this case is to pick the medication option.

There is a further point that needs to be raised. Here is a classroom example every teacher is likely to encounter at one time or another. The teacher has a very disruptive student, and his or her repertoire of fast-thinking strategies to keep the student attentive and in his or her place is exhausted (so is the teacher!). Not only is the student not learning, but he or she is also distracting the teacher from teaching other students. It is time for some serious slow thinking. What to do?

Let us suppose that the choice to continue the situation seems highly likely at 95% to lead to more disruption, which the teacher rates as a −8 and as very unlikely at 5% to lead to a less disruptive outcome, which the teacher values at +4. Then the expected value of keeping things as they are is (.95 × −8) + (.05 × +4) or the sum of −7.6 and .2, which gives −7.4 as the expected value for the no change option.

The other choice, if the student sits with others who egg him or her on, may be to move the student to another desk. Surrounding that student with three or four super-well-behaved students might all but solve the problem.

There is significant potential value to keeping him or her quiet. That student and others may learn more. For purposes of illustration, assign the positive outcome of this rearrangement of the class a value of +10, and assume there is an 80% chance of this outcome happening so that the expected value of this successful outcome is the product of +10 ×.8 for a +8 as the expected value.

However, a potential bad outcome of the move is that there is a 20% chance that the super students may be distracted by the disruptive student's outbursts on occasion. Imagine you have thought about it and assigned a value of −3 to the subsequent likely experience of each of the three surrounding super students, so the total negative value of that outcome is a −9. Then −9 ×.2 gives a −1.8 as the expected value for this bad outcome. When added up, the expected value of the proposed move is the sum of +8 + −1.8 for an expected value of +6.2. So, since the move choice has an expected value of +6.2 and the no change option has an expected value of −7.4, it looks like the logical choice is to move the student.

This is an illustrative example of how decision theory operates, but it may be overly simple in a particular regard. Is the positive expected value of the move choice really sufficient to justify using these three particular students in this way? Is it really fair to them to risk disrupting their education? Are there other factors to be taken into consideration? Answers to these and other questions are part of the debt one incurs when taking on the responsibility to make decisions under uncertainty, *especially if they affect others beyond one's self*. The LFTO challenge demands slow-thinking strategies.

When all outcomes relevant to making a decision are valued by a common standard, economic concerns along with social and personal values, as well as morals of all sorts, can be quantified and aggregated to reach a plausible solution (Weinrich, 2014). Note the word "plausible" here. The word "plausible" indicates the strength and credibility of a conclusion following on the heels of a decision-making process. It also reminds the decision maker that certainty has not been obtained. Slow thinking under conditions of uncertainty aims at securing plausibility and not certain truth.

The tools of decision theory have been used effectively in many aspects of life. Anyone who learns more about decision trees will have gained a useful tool. But keep in mind, decision theory too has its limits. It is but one tool in the menu used to figure things out, and, in the end, it must rely on imagination and must operate through the exercise of critico-creative thinking.

HEURISTICS AND THINKING FAST AND SLOW

Cognitive science is often confused with decision theory. However, there is a line of demarcation between the two, and it is important for any educator interested in critical thinking or teaching critical thinking to know the difference between the two (Gilovich & Ross, 2015). Decision theory is concerned with algorithmic rules for how people should proceed in order to make more efficient and better decisions (Bermudez, 2009), whereas cognitive science focuses on how people actually make decisions.

As economist Richard Thaler (2015) observes, classical economics was based on the assumption that people are rational and self-interested. Fortunately, the failure of economists' predictions of people's behavior shows this is often not the case. When the findings of cognitive psychology were applied to economics, the field of behavioral economics was born. For example, when a person undertakes an unrecoverable cost to punish a greedy stranger, self-interest is typically not the driving force of such behavior.

Cognitive scientists identify *heuristics* that people use to solve immediate problems. A heuristic is a mental shortcut that involves using a simple rule to solve a problem, often by ignoring aspects of the situation. Daniel Kahneman (2013) says people use heuristics when engaged in fast thinking, which is what people do most of the time. When solving difficult problems, people need to slow their thinking and lay aside some of their standard heuristics. Slow thinking, by contrast, is the psychological process that dominates in the Great Conversation. Nonetheless, when it comes to the LFTO, fast thinking and slow thinking both have their places.

Most heuristics are learned through ordinary experience and socialization. These include rules of thumb such as "You get what you paid for" and "If two products are the same, buy the less expensive." People use one or the other of these heuristics when shopping. Each makes sense, for example, when buying jewelry or socks, respectively (Almossawi, 2017). Sometimes, however, they run counter to one another, and there is no fast-thinking maneuver to remedy the situation.

When studying heuristics, cognitive scientists sometimes come across situations in which routine cognitive processes that are often useful instead become ineffective or sometimes self-defeating. For example, one way in which we estimate the frequency of an event is by "the ease with which instances can be brought to mind" (Tversky & Kahneman, 1974). This "availability heuristic" may function well in many circumstances, for example, when we rate the probability of a pride of lions roaming the streets of a large American city as very low because we surely would remember such a thing being in the news.

But, on the flip side, it is a well-known practice of many news organizations to lead their reporting with sensational crime stories, and thus, many Americans believe that violent crime is epidemic in American cities in spite of the FBI data that show a steady decline from a peak around 1991 (Robertson, 2016). These heuristical fault lines in human thinking are important for teachers to recognize and understand. Teachers need to be alert to heuristical fault lines so that they do not contaminate their own thinking and that they can advise students about these common perils in students' developing thinking skills.

For educators one of the more relevant considerations concerns "regression to the mean." Regression to the mean is a relatively straightforward idea. It says simply that when you have more extreme performances, either good or bad, which are affected by multiple random factors, then those performances are likely to be followed by less extreme performances, that is, ones closer to the mean, closer to the average. In sports an outstanding hitting performance in the major leagues is likely to be followed by a poorer performance, one closer to the batter's average, but not necessarily because of any changes the batter makes. A much lower than average student performance is likely to be followed by a better performance whether students are reprimanded or not (Kahneman, 2013).

Anyone familiar with critical thinking is likely to know of the fallacy *post hoc ergo propter hoc*, which means roughly "after this therefore because of this." Kahneman (2013) noticed that Israeli air force flight instructors were convinced that if they reprimanded a student pilot for poor performance in landing his or her plane, the student's performance was likely to improve the next time around, but, if they praised a student for an extremely good performance, the student's subsequent performance would likely be worse. So, the instructors "reached the erroneous and potentially harmful conclusion that punishment is more effective than reward" (Tversky & Kahneman, 1974, p. 1127).

This points out that our repeated experience of pairing of events may not be as revealing of the causes of things as it seems to us. Indeed, Tversky and Kahneman sadly observe that "the human condition is such that, by chance alone, one is most often rewarded for punishing others and most often punished for rewarding them" (1974, p. 1127).

Finally, there are some heuristics that are originally the product of slow thinking, but their use advances the cause of fast thinking. For example, there is the problem of when to stop shopping for a better deal. Imagine you are interviewing for a teaching job. Things are going wonderfully. Nearly every school has offered Juanita a position! When should she stop and say, "This is the school for me!"? How can she be sure that the next school she interviews with will not be a better deal? Decision theorists and computer scientists specializing in artificial intelligence nickname this class of problems the "secretary problem" (Christian & Griffiths, 2016). It is the problem of knowing when to stop a potentially endless search procedure.

The rule that has been recently discovered says, after checking out 37% of the possible alternatives, identify the best. When you next come to one that is as good as or better than the best one in the first 37%, you should select it.

Actual studies have shown this to be an optimal, cost-benefit policy for most search procedures more than 90% of the time. Computers are programmed to use this strategy, and the same algorithm can be used by ordinary people in a wide range of search applications (Almossawi, 2017).

The 37% algorithm is not intuitively obvious. Slow thinking made it known. But once it is known, this algorithm can become a learned heuristic advancing the fast-thinking needs of most people from time to time. The LFTO advises better thinkers to improve both fast-thinking and slow-thinking strategies.

GAME THEORY, VALUES, AND KNOWLEDGE

From the start, it is important to distinguish game theory and a topic currently being discussed in education called "gaming." The idea behind gaming is to create contrived games from board games to electronic games to develop critical thinking. The data for using contrived games to teach critical thinking are not encouraging (Costikyan, 2013). This should be expected. Games only sometimes prompt deep thought. Often, they are for enjoyment only. The dispositional elements of the Great Conversation and the skills of critico-creative thinking are not necessarily prompted by simply playing games.

However, games involving strategic thinking where a player's choices depend on thinking about another player's choices bring us into mathematical game theory reflection and practices (Gerber & Scott, 2011). Such games are promising and in line with adding game theory to a person's LFTO tool kit.

Game theory can sound pretty imposing. The reader should not fear, however. There are many wonderful primers out there if the reader is interested (e.g., Binmore, 2007). Some of the key points in game theory that are intuitively alluring to any critical thinker are briefly noted below. Mathematical game theory is something for teachers to *know about*—especially in the age of emerging STEM curricula. But, there is no need for game theory to be part of the standard repertoire of every teachers' LFTO tool kit (Mei, 2009).

Imagine, as game theorists do, that any social interaction is likely to count as a game. This means only that things can go well or not so well for each of those involved in the interaction *depending on how the other people in the situation behave*. This is the crux of game theory. For things to go somewhat well for everyone involved in a game, it is important to learn what each person in the engagement might want, what each might settle for, and what each would want to avoid at all costs.

People may want many things: material goods, enhanced reputation, better health and fitness, power, social refinement, peace of mind, and so on. Just as in decision theory, game theory is a strategic tool to quantify values and expectations in terms of benefits and costs affecting each player. Solutions can be sought that appeal to all players as a reasonable win-win outcome for all, given the context and alternatives at hand, but there is no guarantee in advance that such solutions exist or can be found (Klarreich, 2017).

Suppose you are taking students on a field trip. For security purposes, students are required to partner up with one other person. Four students hang out together, but one is the center of attention. Each of the other three wants to be that favored person's partner. Think about how each person can wind up at least somewhat satisfied with a reasoned outcome.

When one person's gain can only be at another person's loss, it is called a "zero-sum game." In this case, two of the students could wind up losers and only one a winner, if that one monopolized the favored person as a partner. But if this situation can be framed as a non-zero-sum game, maybe everyone can be somewhat satisfied. Imagine there is a lunch punctuating the field-trip day. Switching partners at lunch ensures one other person gets to partner up with the most popular student. Still that leaves one person out, so it is not a win-win solution satisfying everyone.

One of the most famous scenarios in game theory is the prisoner's dilemma, first framed by Merrill Flood and Melvin Dresher at RAND Corporation in 1950. During the Cold War, game theory was used as a tool to analyze the competition between the United States and the Union of Soviet Socialist Republics (USSR) in the hope of all of us surviving the nuclear standoff, and the prisoner's dilemma was one of the scenarios that was often employed in those analyses.

The prisoner's dilemma is not typical of all of the game scenarios studied in game theory, but it did seem very relevant to the circumstances. The essence of the dilemma is that you have two "players," which may be people but might be teams, organizations, or whole countries. Each player is concerned solely with advancing their own welfare. The players are in a situation where it looks like cooperation would be beneficial to both. However, it might be even more beneficial to cheat.

Let's try to illustrate this with a chart concerned with the efforts of the United States and USSR to negotiate a Strategic Arms Limitation Treaty that would be beneficial to both because creating and maintaining their nuclear arsenals were horrendously expensive. But there is a serious catch, as this little chart will show (see figure 5.3):

		USSR Actions	
		Cooperate	Cheat
USA Actions	Cooperate	Good for USA Good for USSR	Very Bad for USA Very Good for USSR
	Cheat	Very Good for USA Very Bad for USSR	Bad for USA Bad for USSR

Figure 5.3. The Prisoner's Dilemma in International Relations

Let us start from the perspective of the USSR and ask what the smart move is for them in this situation to get the best outcome for themselves. That may depend on how the United States behaves. When we look at the chart with the outcomes specified for each of the two players in the four possible combinations, we find a discouraging result. If the United States cooperates, then the USSR should cheat because a very good outcome is better than a merely good outcome. And if the United States cheats, then, again, the USSR should cheat because a merely bad outcome is still better than a very bad outcome. So no matter what the United States does, the logical thing for the USSR to do is to cheat.

Of course, from the standpoint of the United States, the reasoning is the same. No matter what the USSR does, the United States should cheat because very good beats merely good and bad is better than very bad. And both the United States and the USSR are aware of this mirrored reasoning, so they remain in the box with bad outcomes, when they would both prefer to be in the box with good outcomes.

Historically, what broke the stalemate was the invention of satellite reconnaissance technology. Satellite technology provides enough warning of cheating by the other side to change the very bad outcome to one that was merely bad. For a look at how game theory can be applied, one of the very best places to start is the work of Nobel Prize winner Thomas Schelling (1960, 1967, 1978). Schelling writes very clearly and does not invoke challenging mathematics to cover topics from nuclear diplomacy to how neighborhood ethnic segregation could happen without any sinister motives on anyone's part.

Another scenario that has garnered a great deal of attention lately is the ultimatum game. Its essence is simple, but there are many, many variations on it that have proven inspirational to a number of social science research projects. There are two players, a "proposer" and a "responder," and the proposer has a significant amount of money, let us say $100 as an example, that he or she is to decide what to do with. The rules are quite simple: The proposer is to make an offer to the responder about how to split the money. If the responder accepts the proposal, then both players are given the portions of the $100 that were proposed. But if the responder refuses the proposition, then neither player gets anything.

Start from the perspective of the responder. What if you were offered one penny and the proposer was going to keep the other $99.99? Would you feel offended enough to turn down the proposal with the result that neither of you got anything? Since you passed up getting a free penny, does that mean that there is more than money involved in your decision? Now from the standpoint of the proposer, if you strongly suspect that some offers will be regarded as somehow too low and will be rejected, what split do you propose that maximizes your gain and limits the risk of having the proposal rejected?

Most people in the United States easily see that something close to a fifty-fifty split will make for a proposal that is very likely to be accepted.

Now just begin to imagine the variations that can be tried. Do the two parties know each other, or are they strangers to one another? Do they know anything about the other party like what community or social class they are from? Have they played the game before, and do potential partners get to know their record or not? Does what constitutes an acceptable split vary from culture to culture? If so, why? Would these variations indicate different conceptions of justice or fairness from one culture to another? Would some players who observe the proposed splits "from the sidelines" choose to spend some of their resources to "punish" the players who made unfair proposals? The list goes on. (See Bowles and Gintis [2013] for an overview of this research.)

In complex cases game theorists often use matrixes and equations to work out a solution. In such cases no one gets exactly what he or she wants, but everyone is happy enough with the deal to go along with it, and then there is an equilibrium of realized interests among all the players. These deliberations are ripe for slow-thinking engagement within the Great Conversation. Meanwhile, the simpler examples can help teachers role-model critical thinking to their students (Wagner, 2011).

In contexts of the Great Conversation, game theory underscores the need to learn and slow think about the wants, needs, dispositions, skills, and desires of various cultures, religions, peer groups, social conventions, and economic practices. Game theory emerged from the Great Conversation as a formalized way to bring these considerations together in an attempt to reach an equilibrium point satisfying to all players/participants. The Great Conversation draws together the expertise to sanction strategies such as game theory, algorithms, decision theory, deductive logic, Bayesian statistics, and other tools of higher-level inductive processing. (See Appendix A for an annotated guide to further thinking resources.)

SUMMING UP

This chapter draws attention to some of the most prominent higher-level thinking strategies. Teachers do not need to become masters of any one of them. Of course, inasmuch as teachers should be aware of all the strategies that constitute higher-level thinking, knowledge *about* these strategies is certainly useful.

The psychology of higher-level thinking is as old as the scientific study of psychology itself. Some, such as Piaget, Vygotsky, and Gopnik, have studied how higher-level thinking develops. Others, such as Bloom and his associates, taxonomized what they consider to be higher-level thinking so that teachers and researchers alike might do a better job of focusing on the purpose of LFTO. In this chapter, however, two central points are made that are often overlooked by those studying the above authors for the first time.

First, it is importantly true that there have been numerous advances in logic, computational modeling, statistical theory, and so on that upgrade common inferencing practices of centuries past. The algorithmic aggregation of big data, for instance, has led to insights never before imagined. But even in mathematics, a proof of Fermat's last theorem conjecture, which went wanting for over 350 years, depended on the critico-creative capacity of Andrew Wiles and a few other genius mathematicians and not on high-powered computational processing. In short, thinking excellence in all areas has been enhanced by new computational tools, but computational tools cannot replace the centerpiece of human wonderment and imagination.

Second, each new thinking strategy earns its way to credibility through being reviewed and analyzed in the Great Conversation. The dialogic evaluation of new thinking strategies determines what empirical tests must be satisfied to adopt new thinking strategies in particular cases. The wonderment of critico-creative thinking imagines what algorithmic strategies cannot. Algorithmic strategies must always meet the test of review within the Great Conversation, and the Conversation embraces the entire repertoire of the LFTO thinking strategies.

The Great Conversation is where these plausible truth-finding missions are secured. First and foremost, every participant in the Great Conversation must find a sense of security and skill in dialogic reasoning and critico-creative thinking. Facility in the other excellences of thinking can come later. The way to find one's place in the Conversation is to role-model apt thinkers and to participate in the Conversation personally. Consequently, teachers must learn to participate in the Great Conversation. The scripts in the following chapter bring teachers together in instances of the Conversation in topics of relevance to education and teaching.

As a consequence of participating in the Conversation through scripted immersion in a community of inquirers, teachers advance to capable role modeling for students. There simply is no way to role-model something that a person has not yet developed for himself or herself. The teacher, who has learned through participation in scripted discussion, is a much better candidate to role-model the same for his or her own students one day.

In the moral world, plausibility in managing cooperation, duty, obligation, evaluation of rights, and so on is the ideal. There is no empirical test of confirmation but only rigor of responsible reflective development of ideas and plans. This is secured through following the elements of ethical analysis as enumerated in chapter 3. The toolbox of thinking skills can be quite extensive. First and foremost, however, teachers enter and lure others into effective participation in the Great Conversation by using again and again the two master questions: "How do you know?" and "What do you mean by the term ____?" Every new candidate for thinking excellence must first pass muster in the Great Conversation by measuring up to versions of these two questions.

The pursuit of thinking excellence connects directly with what, long ago, Aristotle wrote about the concept of self-actualization. He saw each person as having a set of personal excellences. The only way to self-actualization was to learn to use one's excellences excellently. From a more contemporary perspective, Maslow (1954, 1970) and Slavin (2015), in the development of hierarchy of needs, placed self-actualization at its pinnacle. To Maslow, self-actualization is "the desire to become everything that one is capable of becoming" (1954, p. 92). In essence, it is a condition of self-fulfillment (Feldman, 2017).

Now, from both Aristotle's and Maslow's perspectives, teachers who model thinking excellence are helping their students achieve to a higher degree their becoming the human beings they are truly capable of being. Is that not a great way to look at life, both for yourself and for your students?

When you learn to use your excellences excellently, you have self-actualized, and you have reliable control over your thinking and your actions in the contexts in which you find yourself (Brighthouse, Ladd, Loeb, & Swift, 2017). In the eighteenth century, the philosopher Immanuel Kant described autonomy as the central goal of education (Jackson, 2011). Autonomy is the capacity to override mere wants and desires and is the ability to make decisions based on good reasons. A few years ago, pragmatically minded educator Phillip Jackson (2011) echoed Kant when he concluded that education should be about developing fitness for the life each student will face—fitness being self-control over the skillful use of one's faculties in context.

Aristotle, Kant, and Jackson are full-bodied participants in the history of the Great Conversation spanning over 2,500 years. Yet on matters of education, each can be seen in one way or another advocating mastery in critico-creative thinking and dialogic evaluation as central to every person's education (Dwyer, 2017). Time now to do some deep thinking on your own. The scripts and the structuring of your communities of inquiry are your development grounds for a self-actualized career in teaching.

Chapter 6

Preservice Teacher Preparation Scripts

As future teachers progress through their training, a deep understanding of their strengths, weaknesses, cultural norms, and learning styles is important to connect with the variety of learners in the majority of today's diverse classrooms. Teachers tend to teach to their strengths, cultural norms, and their dominant learning style.

Possessing a deeper understanding about themselves as human beings will allow them to focus on others and how best to help them learn. The scripts in this section encourage preservice teachers to press the boundaries of their self-knowledge, as well as what they think they know about others and how they learn.

TIPS FOR USING THE SCRIPTS SUCCESSFULLY

- Read the entire script before reading it with your students. This will help you know when you need a dramatic pause or a quick follow-up.
- Be patient with your students! Give them time to think. Many may have never had or had a limited opportunity before to think critically. These opportunities will help move them forward.
- Be slow to give your opinion. Once you jump into the discussion with what you think, the "right" answer has been given, and student thinking and conversation will shut down.
- Wait time! Read a portion of the script that raises a question and wait for a response.
- Use the scripts as often as possible. Although there does not have to be a set curriculum or timeline, the more opportunities the students have to stop and think critically, the more improvements and risks you will see.

- Make this time special. Before beginning the scripts, have the students close their eyes and relax. This lets them know that something different is about to happen. It will seem silly at first, but students quickly begin to enjoy this break.
- Think, pair, and share. Sometimes students are more comfortable having time to write their ideas and sharing them with a partner or small group before sharing with the large group. This is true with difficult topics or when students are just beginning the process.
- Fit the scripts in as an introduction to a lesson. There is no set time for critical thinking. You will find that some scripts will require a longer instructional time. Others are fun and can encourage your students to think critically.
- Reuse some of the scripts at the end of the semester. This way you can really see the development of your students' thinking.

BEAT THEM INTO SUBMISSION

Have you ever heard people speak of a well-disciplined army? Historians describe the earliest Roman legions, as well as the armies of Sparta in ancient Greece, as being very disciplined. They do not mean to suggest that these armies were robotic-like. They do not mean that the soldiers behaved mindlessly. They are not suggesting that the soldiers were in a hypnotic-like state. So what do you suppose people mean when they speak of these armies as well disciplined?

St. Benedict developed what is now known as "the rule" for Christian contemplative orders of monks, lay brothers, and nuns. "What is a contemplative order?" A contemplative order is a group of people with a shared commitment to frequent, private prayer uttered under ceremonial conditions throughout the course of a day. Benedictines and Cistercians are examples of contemplative orders. St. Benedict's Rule is the social law around which each order is centered. People often speak of contemplative orders of priests, lay brothers, and sisters as disciplined.

What do you suppose they mean here by that use of the term "disciplined"?

The term "well-disciplined" can be used to describe and praise armies as easily as it might be used to describe an order of contemplatives. What is the meaning of the term in each case, which makes it the same idea? People routinely speak of disciplined athletes and disciplined students. What are they talking about in each of these cases?

Does well disciplined mean punished often? Does well disciplined mean punished in proportion to one's wrongdoing? Does well disciplined mean conditioning an organism in the manner suggested either by classical or by operant conditioning?

Remember, people have been speaking of well-disciplined armies, monks, athletes, and students long before modern behavioral psychology ever existed. Being well disciplined must mean something other than being trained under another's control. Are soldiers, monks, athletes, and students considered disciplined just because they follow orders?

Apparently not, since we would not use the term if we found out that the candidates for the description were hypnotized or acting other than through free choice. So to *be* well disciplined, one must follow orders because one chooses to do so. But is something more involved?

What if a person is the sort who tries to please everyone all the time? Such a person always follows any order anyone gives him or her. Would you call such a person disciplined? Why not? A four-year-old prankster tells his forty-year-old babysitter to "Go jump in the lake!" If the babysitter does so, would we be likely to call the babysitter disciplined?

In addition to being able to make a choice about what to do, is another feature of being disciplined is that one acts on the choice for good reason? Consider for example that soldiers, monks, athletes, and students may each earn the description, "well disciplined," because there is good reason for what each does.

As described in the poem "The Charge of the Light Brigade" (by Alfred, Lord Tennyson), the British cavalry charged Russian cannon emplacements. Historical reports tell us that, of the nearly 670 men in the brigade, 118 were killed, 127 were wounded, and about 60 were taken prisoners. While the Light Brigade did manage to engage the Russian gunners and temporarily drive them from their positions, the Russian artillerymen were soon able to force a return and to drive the remaining members of the Light Brigade back to the British positions, all the while retreating through murderous fire.

The fruitless charge was described as pompous, arrogant, and most memorably, perhaps, by French Marshal Bosquet as "magnificent, but it is not war. It is madness."

While each cavalry soldier may have been considered well disciplined in his own right, the charge as a whole was just considered reckless—not disciplined. ("Cannon to the right of them, Cannon to the left of them, Cannon in front of them Volley'd & thunder'd.")

How is it that in such a situation, each soldier may be considered well disciplined but the overall charge not considered so? No one is suggesting the charge would be considered *undisciplined*. That would surely be inaccurate. But the charge itself is seen as reckless maneuver and not a "disciplined" strike.

For a person or group of people to be accurately described as well disciplined, the person or people must be making a free choice for good reason, correct? For a self-disciplined person, the *recognition* of what counts as good reason may come from within.

In other cases, a well-disciplined person may act freely on the recognized authority of another. For example, a well-disciplined patient follows his or her doctor's orders because he or she knows the doctor's reasons for giving those orders as they are most probably in his or her best interest. Hence, soldiers have good reason to listen to commanders, monks to abbots, athletes to coaches, and students to teachers. Is there anything more to being well disciplined?

Is the practice of punishment part of the meaning, that is to say, part of the *definition* of discipline? To help people become more disciplined, it is important to have a managed and controlled environment. Punishment may be a tool for insuring control. But punishment is not part of the meaning of control any more than it is part of the meaning of discipline.

Punishment may be a useful device for creating a managed and controlled environment. While a managed and controlled environment may be necessary for developing discipline, just because one thing is necessary for another, it doesn't mean that the terms or ideas share the same meaning.

To help people become disciplined may be a laudable educational objective. For example, it takes a well-disciplined scholar to sustain the rigorous search for truth. But a well-disciplined scholar is not the same thing as a well-punished scholar, right?

To become well disciplined in anything is admirable, but being well punished is not. The close connection between punishment and the kind of environments that eventually leads to disciplined behavior is evident, but that doesn't mean that the one idea translates into the other.

Should teachers seek to make their students disciplined in their studies? What about, in contrast, should teachers seek to make their students well punished? Could a system that has controls, which are too tight, defeat the goal of making its constituents well disciplined? Why is it so misleading to talk of "disciplining" students when what is meant is punishing them?

Is instilling discipline a proper educational goal? Is punishing *each* student a proper educational goal? Explain the difference between discipline and punishment.

Explain the difference between disciplining a student *properly speaking* and punishing a child. Which is a proper goal for education, and which is a proper means?

CHECKS AND BALANCES

How does the system of checks and balances work in the American government? Is this system fragile? Explain your thinking. President Franklin

Delano Roosevelt (FDR) acted to threaten the system of checks and balances because the U.S. Supreme Court found a number of New Deal pieces of legislation unconstitutional. In 1937, his administration proposed a judicial reform bill that would allow him to appoint new members to the Court until he got a decision from the Court that he wanted. This "court packing," as it came to be called, was very unpopular and failed to pass in the Senate.

Then in 1951, the Twenty-Second Amendment was adopted limiting a president's term in office to two consecutive terms because Roosevelt, unlike any president before him, did not follow tradition and give up the office after serving two terms, so he was elected four times. But he died in office in 1945 less than a year after being elected in November 1944. Over two decades later, President Richard Nixon forced one Supreme Court justice, Abe Fortas, to resign to avoid impeachment proceedings and threatened Justice William O. Douglas with impeachment to try to get his way with the Court.

There is also an informal system of checks and balances influencing public opinion. Hollywood, through movies, television shows, stars like news anchors, and selective glitzy news stories, influences the American public. Madison Avenue, those who sell us political candidates, jeans, public policies, and so on, influences public opinion. And finally, teachers when they act in concert through a shared vision influence the public. How well does this system of checks and balances work?

Hollywood (the entertainment/news industry) represents itself. Madison Avenue represents those who pay their fees. Teachers represent what? The good of America?

How effective is the informal system of checks and balances in moderating public opinion? How fragile is this system? What could cause it to fall apart? What are the sources of weakness in this system of checks and balances?

Roosevelt and Nixon are two presidents who wanted Supreme Courts that would rubber-stamp anything they wanted. They wanted this so badly that they were willing to use their power ruthlessly to bully the Court into accepting their will. Clearly, the government's system of checks and balances is no stronger than our willingness to support it.

What if in the informal system of checks and balances on public opinion, one of the checks and balances abrogates its role and just echoes the position of another source of public influence? For example, and more specifically, what if teachers just echo Hollywood by preaching its values? What would this do to the informal system of checks and balances referred to previously?

What can teachers do to keep the informal system of checks and balances operative? More specifically, what can you do as a teacher to keep in balance the turbulence created by those who wish to control public opinion? As a teacher, how many "truths" do you think you have adopted that in fact are not true but represent a myth somebody wanted to create in you and others?

Let's take a look at a few. (Note to script users: All the questions one through twenty-three are rhetorical. Do not solicit responses from participants until the first paragraph following the list is completed.)

1. What's the divorce rate in this country? 50%? Where did that number ever come from? Did you ever bother to ask? Lou Harris went into Internal Revenue Service (IRS) records and found that the worse things ever got was that 70% of all first-time marriages are likely to go the distance. That was in 1986.

   Since that time, divorce rates have fallen, while marriage rates remain stable, so things look better and better. George Gallup didn't believe Harris. He went into the IRS data. He originally thought the 50% rate must be true since it is cited so freely. He found that the worse it ever got was that 60% of all first-time marriages go the distance—well above the 50% party line! He also found that divorce rates declined throughout the 1990s, while marriage rates remained stable. Where did this "truth" come from?
2. Nuclear reactors are safe because there will be an accidental meltdown only once in a hundred thousand years. That sounds very comforting, doesn't it? Do you know what it means?

It means that if you line up a hundred thousand boxes and each year you open one, that one may blow your head off! It could be the one you open this year or the one you open next year or the one you open in 10,000 years. It does not mean that there will be no accidents until the hundred-thousandth year.

Madison Avenue is paid to get people to think the statistic means we're safe for a hundred thousand years. You've heard of a hundred-year flood plain, haven't you? Realtors want you to think that means a flood once every hundred years, don't they? But that is not what it means. It means *on average*, there will be a flood every hundred years.

3. Did you know there were some African Americans who owned other African Americans as slaves prior to the Civil War? Did you know there were slave owners even in the North?

Abigail Adams's (President John Adams's wife) father was a Massachusetts slave owner. Did you know some African chieftains protested the end of the slave trade because of the effect it had on their local economy? Did you know that the divorce rate among African American couples in the 1950s was *less than* the rate of divorce among the rest of Americans during that same period?

4. Did you know that more people now emigrate from the United States to Puerto Rico than those who emigrate from Puerto Rico to the United States?
5. Did you know that in the past twenty-five years, 92% of women doctors elect to do residencies in the five lowest paying subspecialties?
6. Can you name four Nobel laureates? Can you name four Academy Award winners?

Nobel laureates change the world. They give us nuclear power, cure our diseases, and give us the power to understand and reshape the world we live in. Why do you know so little about these people and so much about movie stars? The entertainment/news industry controls the airwaves. They barely mention the Nobel Prize winners. On the other hand, they take whole evenings of prime-time viewing to show us ceremonies in which they give prizes to each other. Is this presentation of their self-congratulatory ceremonies self-serving or a service to the viewers?

7. There is an enormous amount of debate within the scientific community on what brand of evolution is right. (For an exhaustive sampler of the debate, see S. J. Gould's *The Structure of Evolutionary Thinking* [2002].)

For example, Lynn Margulis advocated whole genome acquisition for the origin of some species, Richard Dawkins advocated a gradual tempo arising from the success of selfish genes, and Niles Eldridge advocated a punctuated equilibrium. These are just a few of the different ideas from some of the most famous evolutionists in the world.

Did you know there was so much controversy among scientists about evolution? Let's try another example from biology. Did you know the word "gene" no longer refers simply to a physical item? Today, it is generally taken to mean sequence of DNA that contains a set of instructions.

8. What is a U.S. Supreme Court judge supposed to do? Is he or she supposed to think about how we ought to govern ourselves? Or is he or she supposed to lay aside his or her own prejudices and judge according to his or her most objective sense of what past court rulings say? The relevant Latin phrase here is "stare decisis."
9. Do you know that a federal appeals court has ruled that while women must be allowed to try out for any male sports team, boys are not allowed to try out for girls' sports teams? (The test case dealt with prohibiting a high school boy from trying out for a field hockey team.)
10. Movie scholar and critic Michael Medved and his wife, educational psychologist Deborah Medved, point out that constantly over the past

twenty-five years, the biggest movie blockbusters have been "G"-rated movies. What happened to the law of supply and demand that is supposed to govern market forces?

Hollywood makes dozens of "R"-rated movies for every "G" film. What's that all about? The Medveds point out that without the very generous tax breaks the federal government extends to the entertainment industry, few would attempt to make "R"-rated movies. The financial risk would be too large. The overwhelming majority of "R"-rated movies barely break even.

11. Tom Cruise drives an Audi TT car in the movie *Mission Impossible*. Audi gave the car to the movie company and paid an amount reported to be in the hundreds of thousands to have their car in the movie.

Steven Spielberg recently sold $25 million of advertising to be included in his movie, *The Minority Report*. Have you noticed seeing Coke and Heineken labels displayed more often during the course of a movie? These are not commercials. These attempts at promotional manipulation are in the movies themselves. If people will model stars' use of commercial products, what keeps them from modeling other behaviors as well?

12. Have you heard it reported that humans share 98% of their genes with chimpanzees? What do you suppose people want you to take from that alleged fact? (It is an alleged fact because the scientists are still debating numbers that range from 1% nonshared inheritance to 10% nonshared inheritance.)

It is a fact, an uncontroversial fact, that humans share 25% of their genes with daffodils. Why don't we ever hear about that? Is that important? Does it mean we are 25% daffodil-like? We share 50% of our genes with fish. What that means? It means that we are more closely related to fish than to daffodils in the sense of having a more recent common ancestor.

13. The average life span has increased enormously in America in the past century. What does that mean to you?

Did you know that if you lived to be thirty in 1910, the chances were then that you would live to be seventy-six years old, regardless of your gender? By 1990, if you lived to be thirty, the chances are that you would live to be seventy-eight if you are a woman but only seventy-four if you are a man.

The two big advances in twentieth-century medicine were antibiotics and the near-eradication of mothers and infants dying at birth. Somebody dies at one day old; how many people have to live till seventy-six to get an average mortality rate of forty-two?

The really big question in medicine is perhaps why, after so many years of research, do men who reach the age of thirty have an even shorter life-span expectation now than they had nearly a hundred years ago.

14. Did you know that the leading cause of medical emergencies arising in hospitals is prescribed drug interactions?
15. What is the safest form of travel: commercial airlines or private automobile? In terms of deaths per passenger mile traveled, commercial airlines are far safer. In terms of deaths per trip taken the two modes of transportation are about even. Which statistic do you think is more relevant?
16. Did you know that in recent years the nation's freshman college classes are about 60% women and 40% men?
17. Naomi Wolf wrote in the first edition of her book *The Beauty Myth* (1991) that 150,000 women a year die from anorexia. But did you know that, according to the U.S. Centers for Disease Control and Prevention, the number is closer to 100? By comparison, automobile accidents cause around 40,000 deaths each year.
18. Did you know that it is possible to get AIDS from French kissing if there are any bleeding sores in the mouth? Did you know that no one has ever been cured of AIDS? Did you know that even the drug cocktails given to AIDS patients to extend their lives may one day kill the patients they treat because the drugs are irretrievably damaging to both the liver and the kidneys?
19. Did you know that most prisoners of war captured by Americans were returned to their nation of origin after World War II? Did you know that Americans captured by the Germans had only a one-out-of-three chance of surviving their imprisonment, while Americans captured by the Japanese had only a one-out-of-eleven chance of surviving?
20. Did you know that Moors controlled southern Spain (Al-Andalus) for over 700 years? Did you know that during much of that time, Jews, Moors, and Christians all got along with only occasional hostilities?
21. Did you know that France once controlled Mexico or that, after the Russian Revolution, many Russian Jews fled to Mexico and have remained an active and contributing segment of the Mexican community ever since?

One could go on and on in this manner, but the subject matter of each question is irrelevant to us at the moment. What does matter is whether or not any of these items have ever become a matter of conscious attention for you.

To the extent that you gave little thought to these questions and associated information, why do you think that is?

Do things such as some mentioned previously in any way matter to anything you might think, say, or do as a teacher? How fragile is the informal system of checks and balances that influences public opinion? How important is it for you to develop the habit of asking, "How do they know?" or "What do they mean by the term____?" How important is it to teach and, more important, perhaps, role-model for students a tendency to ask "How do you know?" and "What do you mean by the term____?" What does the expression the Great Conversation of Humankind mean to you now?

How does education (properly understood) help balance the forces of public influence? As a teacher, what's your role in the Great Conversation of Humankind?

DECISIONS/CHOICES

Sometimes in teaching we can be very careless with our talk. This shows up not only in instruction and discussion but also sometimes in the textbooks we use. For example, sometimes people use words as if they are synonymous when they are anything except that. Yet, all too often, when a conscientious student calls the teachers on the sloppy use of language, the teacher ignores it. Think, for example, of the word "choice." What does this word mean?

Now that you know what the word "choice" means, define the word "decision." Are you having trouble distinguishing between the two?

There is a very big difference between choices and decisions. There is a very big difference between making choices and making decisions. What do you think the difference might be?

A pigeon makes a choice and picks one corn kernel and not another. Each kernel is lying side by side. Is the pigeon making a choice? Is the pigeon making a decision? Is the pigeon doing both? If the pigeon is doing both, is there some sequence the two naturally follow?

Two pieces of chocolate lie twelve inches apart on the ground. A column of ants goes back and forth retrieving bits of chocolate from one piece of candy but never going to an identical piece from the same bar of candy sitting twelve inches to the right. Why do you suppose that is? Have the ants made a choice? Have the ants made a decision? Is there a difference between the ants in this activity and the pigeon in its activity? Explain your thinking.

A teacher has two instructional strategies for teaching students about democracy. The teacher picks one strategy to go with, and she goes with it. Did the teacher make a choice? Did the teacher make a decision? Which do you suppose came first: the choice or the decision? Explain your thinking.

Do choices pick out a behavior? Do decisions indicate that some deliberation has taken place prior to action? We can study people's choices from afar as it were; just see what they choose! But to study people's decisions, we have to figure out what might be going on in their mind, in their private deliberative processing, is that right?

There is something called decision theory. It is all about helping people deliberate systematically prior to making a choice. Someone is informed of having a stage four cancer. The person may then sit down and deliberate whether or not he or she should be treated for it. There is no guarantee of getting things right whatever the choice.

In decision theory, systematic conceptual tools such as statistics, decision trees, or sometimes, just making lists and weighing the elements help to inform and to make the best possible decision under conditions of uncertainty. When you teach, you will be called upon to make decisions daily. Would you like to learn to make decision a little bit better? How do you think that can happen? What do you think such instruction would look like?

Ben Franklin famously proposed to a friend to make up a list of pros and cons about marrying a fiancé. Cross off all that equals out. Whichever is the higher score, marry or don't marry, go with it.

Charles Darwin did just that when deciding whether or not to marry his cousin. (He married her.) Lists are fine, but they have disadvantages. Can you list some of the possible disadvantages?

EVERY TEACHER IS A MORAL EDUCATOR

The developmental psychologist Lawrence Kohlberg often explained that every teacher is a moral educator. Kohlberg is unquestionably right about that. Think about it.

Social psychologist Albert Bandura centered his career around the idea that people learn most from others as a consequence of role-modeling. This is especially true, Bandura says, if the person being modeled is seen as a figure of legitimate authority. Do you think he is right? Assuming Bandura's right, do you think this explains Kohlberg's conclusion that every teacher is a moral educator? Explain your thinking.

Kohlberg's insight doesn't really require a great deal of psychological expertise. The nature of teaching itself makes certain things true about its cross-cultural characteristics. Regardless of where one goes geographically or throughout history, certain things are evident about the role of *professional* teachers. Yes, we are speaking here of professional teachers.

Did you forget that teaching, preaching, lawyering, and doctoring are among the four traditional professions? These traditions extend back to the earliest tribal days of peoples from around the world. Not all people who try to teach count as teachers—they never have. Nearly 2,500 years ago, the Classical Greek playwright Aeschylus made fun of people called sophists. Sophists are pseudoteachers. Sophists specialize in talking people into things—whether such things are true or not. By contrast, the truest teachers from whatever time or culture try to avoid teaching falsehoods.

Another thing about professional teachers is that they insist on a certain decorum. True teachers believe that people must be able to listen to one another. Insisting on such decorum goes a long way to modeling the idea of respect: respect of one person for another and respect of all persons for excellence in the search for truth.

Finally, even true teachers inevitably get caught up in culturally bound schooling functions, functions that also have a moral dimension. For example, depending on one's culture, there may be pressure on the teacher to school certain social attitudes into students regarding matters of gender role, patriotism, religion, best form of government, and so on.

These latter pressures stand outside the defining role of what it means to be a professional teacher, but they coexist with the teacher's role in nearly every cultural setting. And, recognizing the power of role-modeling, what choice is there but to conclude as Kohlberg has: "Every teacher is a moral educator."

Regardless of the subject matter you teach, if you prohibit students from hurting each other, from prejudicial speech or action, and insist on civil acceptance or disagreement with another's thought, you are unavoidably role-modeling a whole constellation of moral commitments. Do you think teachers need to apologize for this influence? Do you think teachers have a responsibility to be very careful about what moral commitments they role-model to students? What moral commitments are you willing to role-model for students?

Why is it right to role-model those moral commitments? (Obviously you think those moral commitments are right because if you didn't, then you would not choose those moral commitments to role-model.) Think carefully before you answer. Your answer reflects not only the most foundational commitments you have toward others and to community but also what commitments you sense you are obligated to developing with students.

Every teacher is a moral educator. You cannot avoid such decisions. So now muster the courage you need to take a position that shows you understand that as a teacher, you have both the opportunity and the obligation to bring value into the world. What are, say, two moral commitments that will lead your thinking with your students?

What if the basic commitments you have *as a professional teacher* seem to conflict with the expectations your culture, community, or school has with regard to engendering in students certain attitudes toward others? What should you do?

When the moral aspects of your schooling function conflict with the moral aspects of your educational function, what do you do? (Remember, you have three sets of moral commitments you have to prioritize among: personal duties, schooling duties, and educational duties.)

Imagine you believe that homosexual behavior is sinful. Imagine, too, that your school district has an explicit policy and even curricular lessons aimed at presenting homosexual behavior as socially acceptable. Clearly, this represents a conflict between your personal moral thoughts and your school's official position. I am not going to ask you to reflect upon that at the moment.

Instead, I want you to reflect on whether or not your personal moral commitment about homosexuality conflicts with the most foundational moral commitments you have *as a professional teacher*. In this situation, there is a conflict between a personal moral commitment and a cultural expectation involving your *schooling* function. Do you think there might be a similar conflict between your *educational* commitments and your *schooling* commitments? Explain.

You and the school district have each taken a position on a moral matter. The positions are diametrically opposed to one another, so one must be wrong. There is a serious question about which belief children are to be *schooled* in. Leaving aside the distraction of the particular issue described here, describe more generally how you think teachers should think their way through issues such as this when they arise.

Should people fight? Imagine: two children get into a fistfight on the school playground. Are you under a moral obligation to break it up? Explain your thinking.

Should teachers tell children that it's wrong to fight with one another? Explain your thinking.

Is it always wrong to fight? Imagine a bad person attacks and tries to rape your date, spouse, or friend. Do you think it would be all right for your date, spouse, or friend to fight back? Do you think it would be all right for you to come to your date, spouse, or friend's rescue and fight off the bad person? Do you think you are obligated to come to the victim's defense and physically fight off the attacker? Do you think students should be given access to your thinking in such matters? Explain your line of reasoning here.

We agreed that it is right to stop children from fighting. We also agreed that it is right to teach children about what's wrong about fighting. Finally, we agreed that it is right to fight under certain occasions. So here is the big question: Is it appropriate to teach children that it's okay to fight under certain circumstances? Explain your thinking.

The day after the World Trade Center was bombed, the media interviewed students from City University of New York. Several students said they thought the bombing was wrong, but they wouldn't fight on behalf of their country or city in response to the attack. With smoke from the World Trade Center rising in the background, these students said they thought a military response might be appropriate, but they would never want to be in the military to fight in such a situation.

What do you think about these students' reaction? As a schoolteacher, what should you say to your children about whether or not America should fight in response to the attack?

Do you have an obligation to take a particular position? If you have an obligation in such matters, do you see it as part of your schooling function as a teacher or as part of your educational function? Does it matter whether your obligation is part of your schooling function rather than your educational function? It does of course, so explain why it matters.

If you decide that a schooling function and an educational function conflict, which should have priority as a general rule of thumb?

Do you have a duty to teach children to be patriotic? Would such a duty, if it exists, be a function of your schooling commitments as a teacher or of your educational commitments? Is teaching students that it is okay (or perhaps even obligatory) to fight under certain circumstances the same as or different from teaching them to be patriotic? Explain your thinking.

What is the biggest source of failure to teachers in their role as moral educators? How best do teachers bring value into the world?

EXPERTISE

A long time ago in ancient Greece, there was a very poetic writer who wrote interesting dialogues to present his philosophical thinking. This fellow was also an Olympic athlete. He learned a great deal from his teacher, Socrates. He also taught a great deal to his most famous student, Aristotle.

The Olympic champion whom we are talking about here is named Plato. Plato thought some people were smarter than others. Plato thought some people could know more things than other people could. Does this seem reasonable to you? Can you name some people who know more about some things than you do?

When people know more than you in a special area of thought, is it a good idea to follow their advice in this area? Or do you think you should always ignore the thoughts of people smarter than yourself and just do or think whatever you feel like doing or thinking? Plato thought that when the smart person thought real hard and then discovered a truth, it would be very difficult for the smart person to explain the new truth to those who did not understand or were not able to figure it out for themselves. Do you think this is true? Why?

Plato imagined a group of people in a dark cave. He imagined everyone talking to each other by talking to the shadow the person's body cast on the wall of the cave. So, for example, whenever I talked to you, I always talked to your shadow and never to you. Whenever I did this, you always responded to my talk (you do this by talking directly to my shadow), so we both go happily along our way, each believing we have successfully spoken directly to the other. This is the way we have always done things. And, in fact, this has always allowed us to continue along in this way. Is there any reason why we shouldn't just continue in this way? Explain.

Now, imagine as Plato did that someone turned around and saw the *real bodies* standing in the light. This person now knows that everyone has been talking to shadows all along and not to real people themselves. This person now knows the truth. But imagine this person trying to convince others that they are all talking to shadows and they need to turn around to see the light—to see what is real. Do you think it would be difficult to get people to turn around and see things as they really are? Why? (Or, why not?)

How people are accustomed to talking, their culture, may make it difficult for them to see the truth. Yet, regardless of how people speak, the truth remains what it is. The facts of the material world do not change because of the speech or so-called cultural habits of a group of humans. How is it that some people do see through cultural speech habits? Why is it that newly arrived-at-truth is so hard to share with some people while others seem receptive to novel insights (remember, all come from the same so-called culture in Plato's example)?

Do people sometimes prefer to see what they are used to rather than see the truth? The truth in Plato's example is that people are not shadows on walls but real bodies. This is a real truth, right? To persist in thinking that real people are just shadows on the wall of a cave is to persist in thinking a falsehood, right? So sometimes we think of things that are true, and sometimes we think of things that are false. The more often a person thinks of things that are true in a specialized area, the more likely we are to think of them as experts. Is that right?

Are there experts in physics? Are there experts in the law? Are there experts in economics? Are there experts in medicine? Can you think of times when the experts in any of these fields were wrong? Can a person be wrong about one thing in his or her field of expertise and still count as an expert? So what makes a person an expert? Why is it better to go to a doctor to get medical treatment rather than a first baseman?

How does expertise lead to better decision making? Are there experts in moral decision making? A long time ago, slavery was widespread among human beings and cannibalism was nearly universal. Today, there are laws against each in every nation on earth. For example, the last nation on earth to abolish slavery officially was Mauritania on the east coast of Africa, and it passed a law against slavery in 1981.

When a nation passes a law against something such as slavery, it is declaring that as a public matter, it thinks slavery, or say murder, is morally wrong. If one of its citizens commits slavery or murder, the country then declares the person to be an appropriate target of punishment.

Punishment is a way for the people of the nation to express their moral indignation toward the crime. Punishment also sometimes makes it less likely that such bad things will happen again. Was it a good thing to outlaw slavery? Is it true that slavery is a bad thing?

If most of us changed our minds and said that slavery is a good thing, would it then become a good thing to make other people slaves? Would it be a good thing for other people to make us slaves? Is it true that slavery is wrong, a morally bad thing? Were the first people to recognize the wrongness of slavery in some sense moral experts on this matter?

Plato thought there were moral experts just as there were experts in medicine in the law and in cabinet making. Sometimes even experts get things wrong. But, in the end, those who have thought carefully about certain matters are more likely to be right than most other people who have not thought so carefully. The person who thinks very hard and studies a matter carefully is like the person who looks away from the shadows in the cave and into the real. People who lack expertise continue to look into shadows and think they are dealing with the real.

No matter how many people look into the shadows and agree they are seeing the real, that doesn't make their agreement true, does it? All can agree something is true, and all can be wrong. And, as Plato explained, a single person may look into the light and see what is real, and, even if no one else agrees with the person, that person is still right about what is true and the others are wrong. So some things we say really are true, while other things we say really are wrong. Do you believe this? Explain.

Are there true things about how we ought to treat each other? If there are true things we can say about physics, medicine, and economics, are there true things we can say about matters of morality?

We can be wrong about some things we say in physics, medicine, and economics, but no one concludes that physics, medicine, and economics are just a matter of opinion. Similarly, we can be wrong about some things we say in matters of morality; but why should that lead anyone to conclude morality is just about people's opinions? An expert in physics or medicine is not always right; so what should we expect from an expert in morality?

How do we train an expert in medicine? How would you go about training an expert in morality? What makes you follow the advice of an expert in medicine? What would make you follow the advice of a person you recognize as an expert in morality?

Do you believe Plato is right in thinking that there can be experts in every possible field? What do think of Plato's critics who say, "But who will train the first experts? Where did they get their knowledge? Did they just make it up? Is it all just a matter of opinion? Is it just a matter of where the original trainers were raised?" Are there expert doctors in China? The United States? Chile? Russia? Are there moral experts in Africa? The United States? Norway?

Can American doctors learn from Chinese doctors? Can American doctors learn from Chinese doctors things that are true? Can American moral experts learn from African moral experts things that are true? Can they learn things that are not just believed in Africa by most Africans but that are true for human beings everywhere? Is Plato right about there being real expertise in all realms of life?

What is the best way to learn from an expert? What is the best way to benefit from another person's expertise? Plato learned from Socrates's expertise, and Aristotle learned from Plato's expertise. Have you now learned anything from considering anything of Plato's expertise as a philosopher?

KNOWLEDGE SILOS

Research more than twenty years ago demonstrated that once a medical problem was designated as a gastrointestinal problem, a new computer program could more often accurately identify a patient's ailment better than practicing gastroenterologists. Does that surprise you? Explain why it does or does not surprise you.

Computers can store massive amounts of information, and when the categories of information are well defined, the computer's ability to retrieve information and assimilate it with the information on hand is awesome. But there are things computers cannot do as well as humans.

Analogical reasoning, metaphors, and other imaginative heuristics humans employ are not as readily available to machine intelligence. For example, a gastrointestinal specialist may suspect that in addition to stomach problems, the patient may have other problems. For example, the doctor may recommend to a person with a stomachache that they also have a dermatologist look at a growth on the patient's shoulder. Specialized knowledge is different from generalized knowledge. What is the difference?

A computer program's specialized knowledge does not transfer well beyond its specifications. Humans addressing other humans have sensitivities that are not yet within the reach of programming technology. A teacher may understand that a child's reluctance to learn the parts of a cell today has nothing to do with laziness on the student's part or inept instructional programming. The teacher may know that the child's parents just announced to the child that they are divorcing.

The teacher's psychological knowledge supervenes over the instructional protocol and calls for different teacher responsiveness. Does this make sense to you? Explain why.

Sometimes it appears that the more a thinker knows about a well-defined field, the less able the thinker is to analogize what he or she understands to effectively contribute to discoveries in other fields. For example, the electrical engineer may admit to no knowledge of the cause of stress headaches.

Yet someone less specialized may recognize that stress often manifests itself in headache symptoms and stress may be a function of increased electrical activity to parts of the brain. In this case, the less specialized person may have more to offer the headache sufferer than a genius engineer. Schools are good at developing expertise; but are they as good at developing student skills requiring the crossing of subject matter borders?

Some educators lament that teaching focuses too much on disciplinary focus, maybe to prepare for some high-stakes standardized test. What do you think? These same educators suggest that more attention ought to be given to cross-disciplinary considerations. Would you agree or disagree?

How would you make the curriculum more cross-disciplinary and still optimize effective learning in the standard subject matters?

The world in which we live does not present itself to us in disciplinary fashion. The world is uncertain, and understanding it requires an ability to scan many things that are learned to narrow in and frame a problem space effectively. A real-world problem space is not often defined by math or physics or art or literature. Rather it presents itself to us as a problem for say, raising funds so students can start a soccer club. Think about it.

Would such a problem benefit from a person's mathematical knowledge? Artistic knowledge? Sociological knowledge? Psychological knowledge? Are there other areas of knowledge that might help people effectively address this problem? Give some examples.

When all is said and done, it is the problem which defines the problem space not a subject matter. How can you best teach students to frame problems accurately? How can you best prepare students to optimize solutions to the problems they frame?

Could cross-disciplinary approaches to teaching help address these needs? At the crossroads of all disciplines, people are lured into philosophizing.

Could philosophy too have a proper role in cross-disciplinary instruction? Explain. What are the dangers of a "knowledge silo" approach to curriculum and instruction?

POLITICALLY CORRECT

What does the term "politically correct" mean? We hear this term used all the time, but it seems to be used in a funny way. It sounds like it is expressing a statement of fact, but sometimes it also sounds like it is an act of condemnation.

Let's start from the beginning. Which way do you think it is usually used? Let's begin with a standard way in which people can analyze a term using both an adjective and a noun. Typically, one starts with the noun first since the adjective is only modifying the noun. What does the word "correct" mean?

So the word "correct" means something like *accurate, right*, or *true* to most of you. Some think the word "correct" means just being acceptable to a person or persons in power without having any necessary connection to truth. Do you think that is part of the meaning of the term, or do you think that is how things have evolved because of the way people talk about some things as "politically correct"?

Imagine a group of very young children trying to figure out what the term "square root" means. Imagine specifically that they are trying to figure out the meaning of the term, the square root of 16. Most of the children don't know what they are doing and so they come up with a variety of answers. Finally, imagine one person emerges as the leader because of his or her personality. This person declares that the square root of 16 is 8. The others nearly all agree. Does this mean that it is correct to say that the square root of 16 is 8? Is it really correct to say 8 is the square root of 16, even in this group?

Now, imagine there is one quiet child who doesn't go along with the others. This child explains that the square root of 16 is 4. This child isn't very popular, but everyone knows that this person is smart. The popular person insists on 8. The other children now seem torn. Which answer is correct, 4 or 8? Eight may be a popular answer at the moment, but we all know the answer is 4, right? So 4 is correct even if it is not generally acceptable to the majority at the moment, is that right?

So "correct" seems to mean something closer to true, right, or accurate more than it does "generally acceptable to the majority," is that right? People once thought the world was flat, but that never made the world flat, did it? Most people were incorrect in thinking that the world was flat, and the few who thought it was some kind of round shape turned out to be correct in the end, is that right?

When someone says an idea is correct, the person isn't just suggesting that here is an idea to think about, but rather it sounds as if the person is expressing a fact of some kind that others are supposed to believe. At least, it sounds as if the person speaking or writing is telling others that if they are to have correct thoughts in their head, they should believe this "truth," is that right?

Okay, so when people say some idea is correct, they often expect the matter to end there, with listeners coming to believe the announced truth of the matter. There are occasions when sometimes people do modify the word "correct" with another adjective, and they do modify it for good reason. For example, in arithmetic one plus one equals two. But what happens if you carefully add one drop of mercury to one drop of mercury? How many drops of mercury will you have?

Adding one drop of mercury to one drop of mercury still results in one drop of mercury but with twice the mass. So in talking about the world of mercury, one might be tempted to say one plus one equals one. It is likely that the person would go on to say that in arithmetic; however, it is arithmetically correct to say one plus one equals two. (Most probably, a person would also want to go on to explain what it means to say that the mass of the one mercury drop is now doubled, but that is not relevant to our point here.)

Here the word "correct" may be modified by the adjective *arithmetically* to distinguish this "arithmetical truth" from certain truthful observations people can make in the real world when observing the behavior of something as odd as the element mercury. Is this clear to you all now? Good. That means we are now ready to take on the adjective *politically* as it is used in the expression "politically correct." When we are talking about politics, we are usually talking about what arranges people's relationships within a group, as well as with other groups. This isn't always the case, but often it is.

When people say something is *politically* correct, what do you suppose they are saying? Are they promising or otherwise suggesting that what is said *is* truly correct, accurate, or right? What exactly are people saying when they say something is politically correct?

Do you think people sometimes advise others to speak in a certain way because to do so will likely keep the speakers out of trouble? Do people sometimes use the term "politically correct" to underscore the importance of speaking in a certain way to avoid conflict?

So, in this case, the noun in the term "politically correct" doesn't pretend to name any fact as true about the world, does it? Here we just have a speech act taking place where one person is indirectly advising another to be careful about what one might say to stay out of controversy. Are there other ways in which the term "politically correct" might be used?

Do you know what it means to speak sarcastically? Have you ever heard someone begin speaking by saying that what he or she is about to say is not politically correct, but he or she is going to say it anyway? What is going on here? In this case, the announcement the person makes that his or her statement is not politically correct seems to be an attempt to introduce a real truth as opposed to what everybody at this point is supposed to believe.

Remember the quiet child who knew the square root of 16 was 4? Perhaps he or she would begin telling others this truth by saying, "I know this is not politically correct (since you all believe the answer is 8), but the square root of 16 is, in fact, 4." The person speaking knows others may not want to accept what the speaker is going to say, so the speaker prepares the way by cautioning: "I know this may not be politically correct to say but . . ." Are there yet other ways in which people might use the term "politically correct"?

Imagine a person who is with some friends who want to form a club. Most of the people want to create a gardening club. Imagine the speaker really hates the idea of a gardening club and wants more action. The speaker might say, "It may be politically correct around here to talk about the joys of gardening; but isn't that kind of nerdy? Besides, you can each garden on your own. Instead let's pool our money and get a boat and skis and have a ski club!"

Again, we may recognize some sarcasm here with the use of the term "politically correct." But here the speaker acknowledges—without any judgment of right or wrong—that most people believe a certain thing and yet the speaker wants them to change their mind. In this sort of case, the term "politically correct" is used to make fun of a popular idea in an attempt to get listeners to believe in some other way.

Have you heard people use the term "politically correct" in this manner? Give us an example of such a case. We have listed at least three ways in which the term "politically correct" is used. Can you imagine yet others? With the term "politically correct" being used in so many different ways, do you think this variety often leads to confusion when people talk about something as "politically correct or politically incorrect"?

Do you have any idea about how people might avoid such confusion? Tell us about your ideas for avoiding such confusion. Why do you suppose people allow such confusion as surrounds the use of the term "politically correct" to creep into their shared use of language? Is it important to avoid confusion in language when using such terms? Explain your thinking.

Are you tired of this topic? Do you think it would be politically correct or politically incorrect to speak up and say, "I am tired of this topic!"? Do you think people always know what they are saying or doing when they use terms like "politically correct" or "politically incorrect"? What do you now understand about a term like "politically correct"?

REASON FOR PRIDE

Should students have pride in the educational achievements? What counts as an educational achievement? There are many types of achievements. By definition, each is meritorious. Setting a home run record, great timing when telling a joke, skill at hair styling, and being able to memorize more nonsense syllables than anyone else—each of these is an achievement of sorts; but is any an educational achievement?

Is letting your eyes pass over the works of Plato, Shakespeare, Einstein, Hilbert, or Gould an educational achievement? What if your eyes pass over these works but you don't understand any of them? Does that count as an educational achievement? Educational achievements must involve some sort of understanding, is that correct? How is understanding different from knowledge or information?

Do computers have educational achievements? Computers can acquire information as easily as human beings. One day, computers may be able to acquire knowledge as much as human beings. But most theorists acknowledge that computers could never achieve understanding. Is understanding critical to the idea of educational achievement?

I could be conditioned to do a lot of things. But have I completed an educational achievement merely because I was susceptible to conditioning? Should people be proud of their educational achievements? Why or why not? Can you be proud of something that was unearned? How do you earn an educational achievement?

In 1972, the *Chronicle of Higher Education* reported that major publishers were now requiring textbook writers at the college level to "dumb down" their content and writing complexity to that of a twelfth grader so that college students could read the texts.

In 1976, the *Chronicle* reported that the major publishers had issued new guidelines to textbook authors to write at the level of a tenth grader, since research showed that most college students were no longer able to read twelfth-grade level material.

In 1979, the *Chronicle* reported that publishers again reissued guidelines this time, demanding that authors write at the level of sixth graders (considered the definition of basic literacy) so that college students could read the text. This is the level they have maintained since, although they have encouraged the inclusion of more pictures, cartoons, and so on to keep students entertained along with margin notes to help students remember what they have just read.

In the mid-1980s, over 20% of degreed, certified teachers in the schools of New York City flunked a functional literacy test. That means these college graduates could not read and understand the daily newspaper. In Milwaukee in 1981, high school seniors and their teachers all took the SAT. The seniors outperformed their teachers. What are the grounds for having pride in an educational achievement? Do schools have a duty to provide students a genuine opportunity for educational achievement? How can schools go about fulfilling such a duty?

As a teacher, what can you do to create genuine opportunities for educational achievement on the part of your students? What if the standard curricular materials available to you are not sufficiently rigorous to develop in students a sense of educational achievement? What can you do to enhance the curriculum on your students' behalf?

Which is more of an educational achievement: understanding the concept of entropy or getting an A on a physics test? Can you imagine a person being able to get an A on a test and still not understand the material? Does an A represent an educational achievement in such a case? Could a C ever represent an educational achievement? Describe what counts as a truly educational achievement, and distinguish such achievements from other sorts of achievements.

The average grade point average (GPA) for college students in 1970 was just under 2.4. Throughout the 1970s, average GPAs escalated. This is what is called grade inflation. By 1978, the average GPA had risen to 2.8. Today it is over 3.0 at many schools. Recently, even Harvard admitted it had a problem with grade inflation. It used to be that only rarely did anyone graduate with a 4.0. Today it is quite common. Do you suppose you would be more proud of a 3.5 GPA in 1970 than a 3.9 today?

Leaving aside curriculums such as special education, art, music, and physical education, do you think academic studies ought to be rigorous? What does the rigorous study of a discipline mean to you? Describe a situation in which you would feel a real pride for your academic achievement. Describe what you can do in a class you may teach one day to give students the opportunity to experience rigorous study and the possibility for educational achievement. Is it a professional responsibility of teachers to provide such opportunities?

SAME, FAIR, AND EQUAL EDUCATION

Policy makers often talk about securing an equal education for all. Could that mean an equally bad education? Policy makers often talk about securing the same education for all. Again, could the same education be bad for all? Could the same education be good for all? What makes education "the same" for all? If all schools were brand new and had the same books, technology, and supplies and if all schools were held for the same hours every day, would that be the same education?

Policy makers often talk about securing a fair education for all. What is a fair education? Everyone learns the alphabet, but at one school something happens, and little Billy Shakespeare writes a bunch of plays using that alphabet, and Albert Einstein begins using the arithmetic he was taught to describe riding on a light beam. At the school across town, they learn the alphabet and basic arithmetic, but no students use what they learn to create anything special. Are you really sure they all had a fair education?

What if at one school they had teachers like Socrates and Confucius and at the other school they had teachers like the Kardashians? All teachers taught the alphabet and numbers and such; but do you think different teachers can make the education at the two schools so different?

Is there any way to talk about the same education or equal education or fair education? Aren't each of these ideas different? Explain. Should policy makers start by trying to define education? If policy makers were able to define education, could they then talk about good or bad education? Can education be wholly and reasonably defined? Why or why not? What counts as good teaching?

Will good teaching always look exactly the same between different individuals? If it doesn't look the same, can it still be recognized as good teaching? Explain. How important is good teaching to producing a good education? If an education should be good and policy makers want to be fair about securing good education for everyone, should they start by thinking about the role of good teaching?

Is there any conceivable way policy makers can ensure there is the same number of equally hardworking good teachers in each school? Why or why not? How would you identify and then evenly distribute the good teachers? Do you suppose that some teachers "fit" into some contexts better than others? Explain your thinking. What makes teachers do their best? What can a teacher do in the classroom to make education better for each student there? What is a good education?

SPYMASTERS AND CODES

Militaries and lovers from around the world and across historic eons have been obsessed with coding, especially secret and private coding. Since the twentieth century, computer scientists have specialized in coding. Before there were computer scientists, Britain recruited mathematicians such as Alan Turing and philosophers such as Sirs A. J. Ayer and Stuart Hampshire to work at code-breaking during World War II. In America, statisticians such as L. J. Savage were employed to create unbreakable codes and to decode the attempts of enemies to create unbreakable codes.

Let's pretend we want to create a code for the sentence "Help me." For some reason our code has to use only prime numbers, such as 1, 3, 5, 7, 11, 13, 15, 17, 19, 23, 29, 37, and so on. Take a few minutes now, and create a code system so you send the "Help me" message to a friend who knows your code using only those math symbols. You will need to create a code handbook for you and the receiver.

How does your code work? You and the person you sent the code to each need the same codebook to work from. What are the codebook instructions?

Now imagine you are a code breaker. The coded message above has been given to you to figure out, but you have no instruction book. You only know that sooner or later the code must be translated to English. How might you try to figure out what the secret of the coded message is? What sorts of information would help you break the code? Would it be information about the code maker, information about the symbols used, how long the message is likely to be, if you have seen other coded messages such as this, and so on?

Have you ever been in a conversation with a number of people and you wanted to say something publicly but you really were trying to say something that only your best friend might understand? Were you able to send your message to your friend without everyone getting the true meaning of what you were saying? How did you do that? Was there some kind of unwritten translation code between you and your friend?

Not just computer scientists but many people often try to code a message that is clear on the surface but its meaning is really an entirely different message. How do you code a meaningful message so one set of receivers get one meaning from the message and another set of receivers get a different meaning from the message?

For your secret code to send the meaning "Help me," you created a code in numbers to mean the message in English. How can a code have the same meaning in English and in a sequence of numbers? What sort of thing is meaning that it can be captured with different sets of symbols?

Computers get messages from us in English, code them in some binary mathematical language, and then get back to us with an English sentence we think makes sense. How does that happen?

We know what we mean when we type a sentence into a computer; but where does the meaning go when the computer starts processing its symbols internally? Are the meanings of our sentences roaming around somewhere inside the computer's processing? When the computer puts an English sentence up on a screen, we often think it is meaningful. How did that meaning get there?

The computer codes English into math, processes, and then codes math back into English. At either end we might find meaning; but is there meaning in the mathematical code the computer uses for processing? Is it the same meaning we have when we think about the input sentence? We know how codes work, right? We made one. But how do codes have meaning? What is meaning? How a symbolic system can transfer the meaning humans have in mind?

If a single person makes up a secret code and tells no one its translation rules, can that secret code have a meaning? For a code to have a meaning, do there have to be people who understand the meaning?

Do you think computers understand how meaningful the codes they process may be? Explain.

TEACHABLE MOMENTS

Around much of the world, students were in school attending a variety of classes when news of 9/11 entered their immediate world. This was not something to assimilate in Piagetian fashion. For some, the news may have required attention to restructuring the student's cognitive architecture, so they could, as Piaget would say, accommodate such strikingly unusual news. In any case, the moment the news arrived in every classroom, it became a "teachable moment." What is a teachable moment?

When does a teacher know that a teachable moment is at hand? Certainly not every teachable moment needs to be as astonishing as 9/11; but what are the recognizable contours of a teachable moment?

When a teachable moment occurs, does that give the teacher license to veer from the standard curriculum? Explain why (or why not). When a teachable moment occurs, does that license a teacher to shift his or her instructional strategies for the day or at least an hour or so?

Before the teacher initiates any different tactics of focus on subject matter, do you think students can recognize "teachable moments" when they occur? If students did recognize the opportunity when the teacher is supposed to take advantage of a teachable moment but ignores it, what effect do you think that might have on students' attitude toward the teacher and the school?

Do you think teachers have a responsibility to stay alert to opportunities presented by teachable moments? Is there any way teachers can prepare for the opportunities for instruction teachable moments present?

Imagine one student suddenly lashes out at another student with a racial epithet. After the teacher has calmed down things and order is restored, is the teacher now presented with an opportunity for a teachable moment? Explain your thinking.

Would the subject matter of the class determine whether or not such an outburst presents a teachable moment? Would the aftermath of such an outburst be a teachable moment for a biology teacher as much as it would be for an art teacher? A social studies teacher? Or a language art teacher? Explain your thinking.

If each teacher took advantage of the opportunity for a teachable moment, would they each be likely to address the matter from the same angle, or do you think the context of the different subject matters should influence what and how the teacher might frame the problem space addressed by the teachable moment?

Is it possible to misidentify a moment or a situation as affording an opportunity for a teachable moment? Explain how such a misidentification might occur.

Teachable moments do not present themselves with obvious rubrics and assessment protocols in hand. Does that make teachable moments less important than standard well-structured classroom protocols?

How might a teacher mismanage a teachable moment? Do you think having access to a script such as this that addressed some aspect of the situation might be of some benefit to the teacher? Explain why that might help or might not help.

How important do you think teachable moments can be to helping students achieve higher-level thinking skills? How important do you think the masterly management of teachable moments is to creating a truly good education for students? Explain why you think as you do.

TEACHER VALUES

Should teachers impose their values on students? Do teachers have a right to impose their values on students? Where do students get their values from? Where should teachers get their values from? Explain your thinking.

Are some values better than other values? Explain. Are all values the same? Explain. Are values just a historical accident of the culture one is in? Can one value doing wrong as well as value doing right? What is the difference between the two sets of valuing?

Psychologist Lawrence Kohlberg said every teacher is a moral educator. What do you think he meant by that? Is it possible to be a teacher and not be a moral educator?

As soon as you settle in to teach students reading, writing, or arithmetic rather than, say, how to torture kittens, are you not imposing values on them? Is it right or wrong to impose such values on students? Explain your thinking.

Teachers also tell students to raise their hand if they want to be called on or stay in line when walking through school halls. The students may not want to raise their hands or may not want to walk in line. Their values in these matters are different from those of the teacher. Should this matter? Whose values should matter more in these cases, the teachers or the malcontent students? Explain your thinking.

Some students may think other students are ugly, and they say so. They value this act of free speech. Do you value protecting this act of free speech, or do you step in to stop such verbal bullying? What gives you a right to stop such verbal bullying?

What if your society said certain ethnic groups have no right to public education? This very thing happened in the 1930s in Germany. What is the right thing to do: to follow the government's directive or to try to include the children in class? How do you justify this decision?

Do you value the search for truth? Do you think students should value the search for truth? Explain your thinking. If a teacher did not value the search for truth but a student did, does the teacher have a right to try and discourage the student in seeking truth? Why or why not?

Is Kohlberg right in saying that teaching by its very nature is a value-laden process? Explain your thinking. Do teachers have an obligation to figure out what are the right values to impose or encourage in children? Explain what the basis for that obligation is.

Is encouraging students to seek truth an inherent part of education and hence teaching itself?

Do teachers have moral obligations to students? What are some of those obligations? What makes them obligatory? Do teachers have obligations to the student's parents? What are some of those obligations? What makes obligation to the student's parents so obligatory?

Do teachers have obligations to principals and to the government? Are there ever grounds for ignoring the obligations you describe to principals and government? Explain your thinking.

Do teachers have an obligation to secure respect for the credibility of a subject matter being taught? What are the grounds for that obligation?

Does it make any sense to say teachers should be value free in their professional life? Explain your thinking.

THE DOGMATIST AND THE TRUTH-SEEKER

Rodney the relativist is very proud of himself. He has figured out the answer to one of the biggest questions ever. He boldly announces his new answer to his friend, Trudi the truth-seeker. Rodney declares, "Trudi, guess what I've figured out. There is no right or wrong, no true and false! Nobody can tell anybody else what to do or what is right or what is wrong for that person. It all just depends on how a person was brought up! It's a cultural thing."

Rodney is just beaming from ear to ear. He is so smug about having such knowledge. Trudi is Rodney's friend. She tries to be patient with him even though she knows he is something of a braggart who always thinks he has *the* right answer to everything. Trudi thinks about what Rodney says, and then she says finally, "Rodney, how do you know that? How do you *know* that truth is all relative?"

Rodney is easily unsettled around Trudi because his experience over the years has been that when Trudi asks questions, there is usually a powerful point behind them. Rodney sometimes self-consciously teases Trudi by calling her "Socrates."

Just like Socrates's questions, Trudi's questions often have powerful insight hidden behind them. Now that Trudi has asked Rodney how he knows what he has just stated, Rodney is worried. So he asks Trudi in return, "What do you mean, 'How do I know?' Trudi, what do you think you know?"

Trudi smiles in an understanding fashion. Rodney is in a tough spot already, and he cannot figure out a way to get loose of it. So Rodney is going to try to get Trudi to say she knows something. He figures that if he can get her to say she knows something and, he can show she doesn't really know it, he won't have to answer her question to him about what he knows. In this way Rodney figures he can avoid answering Trudi's question about how he can *know* that "truth is all relative."

Unfortunately for Rodney, Trudi is just too smart to be lured into such a trap. "Rodney," Trudi says, "we are not talking about anything I know or don't know. *You* were the one who announced something you claimed to be true. *You* were the one who said you know that nobody can know anything. *You* said everything just depends on how a person was brought up. So, Rodney, the question at issue is 'How can *you* know what *you* are saying is true?'"

Rodney stumbles around a bit and repeats his original "truth." In other words, Rodney simply declares that in different societies people see things differently. He presents no evidence and no argument to make his "truth" at all compelling. Trudi isn't tricked by such a clumsy maneuver. When Rodney is done repeating himself and declaring his position to simply be true, Trudi patiently responds, "Rodney, *you* still haven't explained how you *know* that what you are saying is true."

Rodney, scared and frustrated, says, "What do you mean, Trudi? I thought I had."

Trudi explains, "Rodney, you are claiming to state a truth. The truth you want to state is that 'all truth is relative.' But Rodney, think about it. If you are right, then you must be wrong. If you are wrong, then you might be right. If *all* truth is relative, then your statement must be relative. If your statement is relative, then it cannot be a statement about *all* truth, as you claim. Rodney, you are in the middle of a paradox. Again, if all truth is relative, as you say, then your claim must be relative too."

Trudi goes on to explain further, "If all truth is relative, then there is no reason to believe what you say about the relativity of truth. On the other hand, if you are right, then it is not the case that *all* truths are relative. This is because you intend the statement you are making to count as a truth, and so some truths would not be relative. The problem here is that when you say there are no culture-free truths, you make it impossible for what you say to be necessarily true across all imaginable cultures. You cannot have it both ways, Rodney. Either there are culture-free, that is, cross-cultural truths, or there are not. Which is it, Rodney?"

"But, but," Rodney stumbles, "prove to me there are truths!"

Trudi can't hold back a smile at this point, "Rodney, I don't have to prove anything. I am not making a claim to know anything; you are. My questions ask only that you show how you *know* what you claim to know. If you can't make good on your claim to know, then there is no reason for anyone to agree with you that 'truth is all relative.'"

Rodney rudely interrupts, "Aha, so you think there are truths!"

"Rodney," Trudi exclaims, "try to stay focused here. You claimed to know something. Our discussion is solely about what you claim to know and nothing else. My question led you to see that your very claim to know contradicts itself. It cannot be the truth that *all truth is relative*, and, at the same time, *your 'truth' is not relative*. You can't have your cake and eat it too."

"Well, Trudi," Rodney cries, "maybe there is just one truth, and I found it!"

Trudi replies, "Certainly, Rodney, it would be wonderful if you and you alone found the one truth that exists, namely, 'all truth is relative.' But again, Rodney, think about it." "How likely do you think it is," Trudi asks, "that you found the only nonrelative truth? More important, and to return to the point I keep making, all that matters in this discussion is the strength of your claim that 'all truth is relative.'"

(Rodney nods in slow agreement). "Rodney," Trudi continues, "You have not made good on your claim to know. So, at this point, I have no reason to agree that all truth is relative."

"Do you think all truth is absolute?" Rodney interrupts.

Trudi explains, "Rodney, I never said such a thing. It makes no sense for you to ask such a question since all that is at issue is what you claimed to know."

Rodney moans dejectedly, "I hate to admit it, but I do seem to have quite a problem here. Changing the subject, can I ask what you think about truth?"

"Rodney, it's hard to say." Trudi explains further, "I am not as dogmatic as relativists tend to be. I am a truth-seeker. I keep looking for better and better answers to the best questions I can imagine or the questions others share with me. I don't know that I would ever recognize cosmically grand truth even if it fell right into my lap.

"I do think the more I think, the more I study, and the more I talk to other sincere, truth-seeking people, the further I move from error and toward truth, truth in lots of matters. I also suspect that there are several types of 'truths.' Some truths we hold tentatively until something better comes along, and others we *may* hold universally. These so-called universal truths are true across a population or discipline at a given time. For example, the 'truths' of mathematics hold for as long as people do that sort of thing."

Trudi continues, "Are the truths of mathematics *absolutely* true? Presumably we mean by 'absolutes' truths that are true across all populations and across all historic epochs. Rodney, I couldn't even speculate about such a thing. A person would need to have a godlike mind to know about such absolutes. I don't. Do you?"

Finally, Trudi concludes, "In any event, Rodney, unlike the dogmatic relativist, I am not so concerned about running around telling others I know things like 'truth is all relative.' Instead, I spend my time finding the most plausible truths for doing science and living life. I never seriously or rationally doubt that truth exists. Consequently, I never end my search for truth. I hold all truths tentatively. But that does not mean I think truth is a tentative sort of thing. It just means I recognize human limitations. We do not have godlike minds. We are prone to error."

"On the other hand, we do some pretty good thinking sometimes, and we'll get better at it if we keep trying. Unlike the relativist, I am not going to stop and proclaim truth. Rather, I will stay on the go, always looking for a better understanding of things. Gosh, that's a lot of talking for me. Sometimes, Rodney"—Trudi giggles—"you bring out the worst in me."

Keep the example of Rodney and Trudi in mind and consider the following:

- What does it take to genuinely be a truth-seeker?
- Why do you suppose some people can be so obstinate when declaring their self-anointed truth that "all truth is relative"?
- Since there is no argument to prove that truth is relative to culture or where and how a person was brought up, does that suggest that people who declare such beliefs to be true have been indoctrinated?

You can persuade people by asking a well-timed question. A well-formed question can reveal whether or not there is sound argument and evidence in support of a claim. But a question, by itself, can never justify a claim to know. Remember when Rodney was asked how he knew all truth is relative? Once he stopped simply repeating his claim using different words, he tried to win his point by forcing a question on to Trudi. Unfortunately for Rodney, Trudi was smart enough not to fall victim to that kind of trap. A question can never prove a claim. A question can only reveal what is missing from a claim. Since Rodney was making the claim in dispute and not Trudi, there was no reason for Trudi to answer the distracting questions Rodney unfairly posed.

There is so much we don't know about medicine and the human body. But the "truths" we currently hold tentatively are helping doctors to save more lives than they were able to a century ago. Doctors don't know any cosmically grand truths, but they sure have eliminated a lot of error from their thinking of a hundred years ago. And, of course, there is so much more to learn. Isn't this the sort of attitude we should be instilling in students during the course of their education?

Whose education do you think served each person better: Rodney, whose education turned him into a dogmatic relativist, or Trudi, whose education turned her into an earnest truth-seeker? How do *you* know when you have been indoctrinated? How can you tell when you are indoctrinating your students? Can you unintentionally indoctrinate your students?

Why is it so difficult for people to maintain focus during an intellectual discussion? Do people today lack a thirst for truth? Are people today too willing to accept the claims of others based simply on the other person's personality? Do you think people today have a proper respect for real intellectual expertise?

The most famous Spanish philosopher of the twentieth century, Ortega y Gassett, thought people had lost a sense of respect for scholarship and expertise. He thought we are too quick to discount expert opinion as "just opinion." What do you think? Are people today too interested in getting their own point across rather than really understanding the ideas of others? Ortega thought that, for many people today, when an issue becomes difficult to understand, they just opt for a solution *they like* rather than one that addresses all the elements of the original issue. Again, what do you think?

Do you think it is possible that the longer some students stay in school, the more they lose their hunger for truth and thirst for knowledge? Explain.

What is the difference between an *argument* in support of a claim and the mere expression of *an opinion*? Belief and truth are not the same thing. How are they different? Knowledge and truth are not the same thing. Explain how they are different. Belief and truth are usually thought of as key to justifying one's claim to know. How are belief and truth related to knowledge?

Is the opinion of an oncologist regarding whether or not you have cancer more likely to be accurate than the opinion of a bricklayer? Can some opinions be better than others? How do you know some opinions are better than others? Why should you allow yourself to be more persuaded by some opinions more than by others? Is the truth better than mere opinion? Is it a good idea to seek truth and not just settle on what some other people happen to believe? How do you seek truth?

THE POINT OF EDUCATION

Is there a purpose to government? What is *the* purpose of government? Imagine each of us is a medical doctor. Now imagine, too, that a sociologist asks each of us what our respective purpose is in being a doctor. One of us may respond, "It's to make a lot of money." Another may respond, "It's to make my parents happy," and yet another may respond, "I do it for the prestige."

After polling each and every one of us, the sociologist has a list of purposes. Some of the purposes may show up more than once, so the sociologist may be able to publish a statistical breakdown of the purposes; we, as a group, identified as our collective purposes for being a doctor. Such data may be very interesting, but none of it tells us anything at all about *the purpose* of the practice of medicine itself.

Regardless of the purpose of individual physicians, the purpose of medicine is to heal the sick and injured. Some individual doctors may do it more conscientiously than others and some better than others, but no facts about individual doctors or even sociological facts about groups of doctors speak to the philosophical question: What is *the purpose* of medicine? (Or in other words, what justifies the practice of medicine?) So the purpose of the practice of medicine is to heal the sick or injured, and this purpose gave rise to doctoring throughout the world and continues to justify its existence even today.

Similarly, something must have given rise to governmental organization. The fact that individual governments may have different purposes tells us no more about the purpose of government than the fact that individual doctors may have different purposes for practicing medicine. Medicine has a purpose quite apart from the individual purposes of practicing doctors, and so, too, government has a purpose quite apart from the individual purposes of actual governments.

So now, let me ask you, what appears to be a similar question: Does education have a purpose? What is the purpose of education? Is there more than one purpose to education? What is propagandizing? Is the purpose of propagandizing different from the purpose of educating? Explain.

What does it mean to "socialize" someone? What is the purpose of socializing a person? Is the purpose of socializing someone different from the purpose of educating someone? If the purpose is to socialize a person, is there any reason to worry about *truth*? If the purpose is to educate someone, is there any reason to worry about *truth*?

A distinction is routinely made between schooling practices and educational practices. Examples of schooling practices may include requiring students to raise their hands when they want to speak, walking in orderly fashion through the halls, collecting milk money, saying prayers, and showing honor to certain adults, especially dignitaries. How does all this contrast with educational practices? What are some examples of educational practices?

In schools all around the world, teachers are held responsible both for schooling practices and for educational practices. Should professional teachers prioritize one over the other? If you must prioritize one over the other, which priority should be accorded the highest ranking? Explain your priority. What is the purpose of schooling? Is the purpose of schooling different from the purpose of educating? Is the purpose of schooling most similar to the purpose of educating or the purpose of socializing?

By this time, you may have noticed we do not have a clear definition of the purpose of educating. To say that something has a purpose is to acknowledge that it is done for some higher end. Medicine is done to achieve the higher end of restoring people to health. Government, too, exists for some higher end. Presumably, schooling and socializing have purpose. That is to say, each presumably has some higher extrinsic end outside itself that justifies its practice.

But now here's something surprising. Two very famous political theorists, R. S. Peters and Michael Oakeshott, each wrote that education has no higher end outside itself. What do you suppose they meant?

Interestingly enough, Plato, too, thought that education, for those most capable, had no higher end. And similarly, Aristotle thought that for the self-actualized person, education has no higher end. What could all these people mean by the idea that at least in some cases education has no higher end?

Ancient Jewish Talmudic commentary makes a distinction between training and education. The Greeks and Chinese, too, made this distinction. The distinction was fairly widely honored until 1892 when at the world's fair, the United States announced a new practice it called "vocational education." Now surely the ancients would think a term such as "vocational education" amounted to a contradiction in terms, or at least, constituted something of an oxymoron. Presumably, Peters and Oakeshott would think so, too. What do you think?

Peters and Oakeshott think education has no higher purpose *because it is an end in itself.* Education, they say, has no higher purpose beyond itself. What do you suppose they mean by that?

Things that are done for some other end have only *instrumental* value. They are pursued only because of the value they can bring about. For example, medicine brings about the higher value of health, so the value of medicine is instrumental. It is instrumental to the end, goal, purpose, or higher end of bringing about human health. Do you think education has a higher value that justifies why it is done, and is the value of education, then, solely an instrumental value as well?

Is there a higher end, goal, or purpose that justifies the practice of education? If so, then what might that end be? Could education itself *be* an end in itself? If we speak about education as the Great Conversation of Humankind, how does that notion fit in with your thinking about education thus far? If education is participation in The Great Conversation of Humankind, does education have any higher purpose?

Can education be both an end in itself and have instrumental value as well? Explain what you think justifies the practice of education. What is the role of the teacher in education? How should a professional teacher prioritize between matters of education on the one hand and matters of training, schooling, and socializing on the other?

Some say it is the duty of teachers to guard the practice of education. Do you think that is true? How could a teacher "guard" the practice of education?

As a *professional* teacher, what are your responsibilities? Give an example of a common failure of professional responsibility among teachers today. Give an example of a common failure of responsibility on the part of other educators today (administrators, counselors, etc.). What is the most important thing you can do to keep yourself focused on your responsibilities? What makes you think this will help you keep your focus?

As a *service* profession, teaching focuses on the well-being of others. How do professional teachers, *as teachers,* enhance the well-being of others? Since teachers focus on the well-being of others, their actions are highly moralistic. They necessarily and inevitably involve value judgments about what is in the best interest of others. As a professional teacher, what do you feel you are obligated to do for the benefit of others?

In what sense are you duty-bound to your students? In what sense are you duty-bound to seek objective and shared understanding of a subject matter?

Are you duty-bound at times to create in students a passion for truth (some call this "a questioning attitude," but that may not be the same thing)? Are you duty-bound to arouse doubt and uncertainty in students? What do you owe to the subject matter you teach? What do you owe to colleagues, supervisors, parents, and the community at large? How would you prioritize your various duties? Why should a person want to be a teacher? Why do you want to be a teacher?

THE TEACHER OF GOOD THINKING

Questions to think about:

1. What does it mean to be a *critical person*?
2. What does it mean to be an *analytical thinker*?
3. Is there a difference between *being* a critical person and *being* an analytical thinker? Explain your thinking.
4. Could analytical thinkers appear sometimes to be critical of others? Explain how that could happen.
5. Could being an analytical thinker lead naturally to becoming critical of other people?

6. Could being a critical person lead one to become an analytical thinker in most cases?
7. Explain again what the difference is between being a critical person and being an analytical thinker.

THINKING ABOUT MORALITY: SOME OPEN-ENDED QUESTIONS

1. What is a good person?
2. What is a moral expert?
3. Is tax law ultimately grounded in moral considerations?
4. Is the *source* of moral motivation found in people's souls, their genes, the human species, platonic forms, some kind of divine absolutes, community, family, some combination of the above, or something else altogether?
5. It is argued that chimpanzees share as much as 99% of the human genome. To what extent does that mean they share in the human moral experience, that is to say, the human sense of morality?
6. Gang leaders and surgeons both use knives to penetrate the body of another human being. In each case, death is sometimes the result. The gang leader may kill to secure power or obtain revenge against a rival. The surgeon is trying to save the life of the person he cuts. Sometimes things just don't work out as the surgeon planned. The surgeon's experience is written off as a matter of fate or an accident. The gang leader's killing is called murder. Is murder profoundly wrong? Or is the act of murder just unconventional within a given society? (Keep in mind that murder is killing with *malicious* intent.)
7. How are personality traits and character traits generally different from one another?
8. Are animals, including the human animal, motivated solely by self-interest?
9. What is a vice? Give an example of a vice.
10. List four universal virtues.
11. Sometimes the most unfair thing we can do is treat everyone equally. Explain why that is so and then define the word "fair."
12. Is there a duty to refrain from harming others? Do people have a right not to be harmed by others? What is the relationship between duties and rights?
13. Do you have an obligation not to cause malicious harm to another person? Do you have *an obligation* to be charitable toward others? What does the word "obligation" mean?

14. To think effectively as a moral agent, how important is it to have an exact understanding of moral terminology?
15. What does it mean to say that the law is just that subset of morality that those who hold the sovereignty of state wish to endorse and enforce?
16. Is there any *necessary* relationship between morality and religion, generally speaking?
17. Even in mathematics we make assumptions before thinking about mathematical matters. These assumptions are called axioms in mathematics. Euclidean geometry, for example, begins assuming the truth of standard logic and five geometrical axioms. Non-Euclidean geometry has only four axioms. A famous logician, Kurt Gödel, demonstrated that no number system can justify its truth from within its own system. This fact is often described by saying that Godel showed every number system to be necessarily incomplete. Physics employs the axioms of mathematics and adds further axioms about the nature of matter and energy. Each of the other sciences does the same. In short, every science begins with assumptions. More generally, one can say that no one ever thought about anything without first making assumptions. Is there any good reason to think that moral thinking is *necessarily* more subjective than thinking in the sciences or thinking more generally?
18. Which is more important: to respect a person or respect a culture?
19. Slavery was once widespread among the human species. Now, every nation on the face of the earth has formally outlawed slavery. Still, there are a few places where slavery continues and the laws of the land are not enforced. Nevertheless, slavery is nearly universally condemned just as are murder and incest. Does this represent a *moral* advance? What counts as a moral advance?
20. Currencies such as dollars, yen, francs, marks, and pesos do *not* exist in the way rocks, water, and wind exist. Yet dollars can be a proximate cause of a dam or its demolition. The whole idea of currency is an innovation of the human species and now functions in a proximately causative way in the world. What enables something to count as a currency? Some would say that the greatest invention of the human mind was not the control of fire or creating the wheel but rather the invention of the promise. Promises make marriages, banking, business, and all sorts of relationships and activities possible. Promising is a matter of placing a person under obligation to another. Promising, whatever else it might be or however it might be enforced in certain circumstances, is, at its most fundamental level, a moral innovation. What does the practice of promising tell us about the moral nature of human experience?

Chapter 6

TRUTH-TELLING

What does it mean to "tell the truth"? If it is possible to tell the truth, then it must be possible to tell something that is not true, is that right? If a person deliberately tells another person something that is not true, what is he or she telling the person?

People sometimes lie or find other ways to deceive each other, so either a person can hide the truth or a person can reveal the truth. What other sorts of things can be hidden?

What sort of thing is truth? Obviously, truth must be the sort of thing that can be hidden from others, and it is the sort of thing that can be revealed to others. With that knowledge about truth in mind, how would you answer "What sort of thing is truth?"

Now that we have some sort of idea about what truth is, can you tell me what truth-telling is? Does "truth-telling" *always* involve an intention to be honest? Explain. If truth-telling involves an intention to be honest, does truth hiding involve an intention as well? What intention is involved when a person tries to hide the truth from others?

Long ago a lot of people thought the world was flat. If asked about the shape of the world, these people would say, "It is flat." These people were not reporting the truth. On the other hand, these people were not lying. In no way were they trying to hide the truth from others. They just didn't know what the truth was. It was something of an accident that they spoke falsely about the shape of the world. They didn't know what the truth was. They simply believed something that was actually false to be true. When asked what their intentions were in saying the world is flat, they would presumably say, "We intend to tell the truth."

So is intention a part of truth-telling? Explain. Can intention be a part of truth-telling but not a part of the truth itself? Explain what you mean. Is intention a part of lying or otherwise trying to deceive others? Is it possible to lie accidentally? Explain your thinking.

Shakespeare said that a rose by any other name smells just as sweet. Shakespeare thought it was true that roses smell sweet. His intention was to tell the truth. But telling the truth isn't the same thing as knowing the truth, is it? Why not?

Why does truth-telling involve intention? Why does the definition of truth itself not require reference to anyone's intention? Truth and truth-telling are two separate things. What is the difference between the two?

A person can sincerely be telling the truth but get things wrong, correct? Isn't this what happened when some people were telling others they thought the world is flat? The *truth* itself, however, cannot be wrong or false, can it? Wrong or false designates the opposite of truth, does it not? When truth-telling, a person aims at the truth, right? A person may aim at the truth, but they might miss the mark and not report the truth accurately, is that right? So what is the difference between truth-telling and the truth?

(See Michael Lynch [2004] *True to Life: What Truth Matters*.)

UNINTENDED CONSEQUENCES AND EXPONENTIAL GROWTH

In one story about the origins of chess, a wise man from India by the name of Sessa invented the game of chess in India long ago. He presented it to the maharaja as a gift. Delighted, the maharaja told him he could have any reward he liked. Sessa claimed to be humbled by the reward and asked simply that a grain of wheat be placed on the first of the sixty-four chessboard squares. After that he asked the maharaja to please double the number of grains until there have been sixty-four doublings—the same number as the number of squares on a chessboard. The maharaja sent his accountants to tally the reward. What do you think happened?

The accountants eventually told the maharaja that the amount of grain owed exceeded all that was then in the kingdom. The maharaja then had Sessa beheaded for his trickery. The maharaja agreed to what he thought was a modest reward. The exponential growth of doubling grain each time produced an unintended outcome for the maharaja. But it was what he agreed to with Sessa. How can people avoid making mistakes like the maharaja's? What is an unintended consequence? When are unintended consequences avoidable? When are they not avoidable?

Howard Wainer (2016) is a statistician who has published more than 400 papers and twenty-one books. He once proposed the following problem frame:

You won a lottery, but you must choose your prize from two options. They are:

1. you get $10,000 a day for a month or
2. you get a penny on the first day of the month and that amount doubles every day for the month (pp. 14–15).

Which option would you choose? Explain your choice. Which option do you think most people would choose when given these two options?

As Wainer explains, after ten days, choice one gives the winner $100,000 and choice two only produces $10,485.75. Yet keep doubling as option number two prescribes, and see what happens! At the end of thirty-one days, option one produces a total reward of $310,000. But option two produces $21,474,836.47. This happens because of the doubling effect, or what is called exponential growth. Do you think people can learn to be on the lookout for the consequences of exponential growth?

Describe some thinking skills that you think might help people be more alert to making the best decisions in cases such as the previous two. Describe some thinking skills that you think might protect people from harmful unintended consequences.

Can an unintended consequence ever turn out to benefit a person? How can that happen? If sometimes unintended consequences can turn out to be good, does that mean we should not worry about unintended consequences?

Can you give an example of how an unintended consequence once affected your life? Can you explain what you might have done to become alert to the unintended consequence before it occurred?

WHAT IS EDUCATION?

We *train* doctors, lawyers, engineers, military officers, and other highly paid professionals. We *train* professional philosophers and astrophysicists. The first group is smart and, usually, wealthy and widely esteemed in our communities. The second group is made up of wicked, smart intellectuals who are often respected in our communities as well.

However, being trained is not an attribute that makes one a member of the elite. Welders, soldiers, and technicians of all sorts are trained as well. Any variance in income or community esteem has nothing to do with whether or not people were trained for their positions. What is training all about? Training and education are different. *Rubrics* are critical to training folks. Can you explain why?

Philip W. Jackson began the twenty-first century by echoing a question addressed by Confucius, Plato, Immanuel Kant, John Dewey, and others. He asked simply, "What is education?" (Jackson, 2011). So let's start by answering Jackson's question. What is education? How is education different from training?

We can measure the success of trainers oftentimes by measuring what their trainees can do in line with the rubric of instruction. But educators might have a different task, so a different understanding of success might be appropriate. Do you agree? Explain your thinking.

Is education just about instilling demonstrable skills in students? Is education a matter of preparing students to respond predictably to recognition test items? Should the effect of a good education lead students to ask penetrating questions as effectively as they can deliver answers to well-formed problems?

What exactly does it mean to "become educated"? Does being educated mean a person no longer has to learn? If a person thought he or she no longer needed to learn, would that count against his or her being properly described as educated? Explain.

Regardless of the range and depth of one's education, does being educated require that the person described be inclined to seek ever more plausible answers, thereby approaching some ideal of truth? What if a person didn't care about truth and instead always said, "That's just the way I (we) do it"? Would that count against the person being described as an educated person?

Would it make sense to say that rubrics are suitable for training programs because they prescribe protocols, practices, and policies that are explicit and well known to all competently trained individuals? In contrast, education involves much that is treasured and valued for a variety of both social and individual reasons. Moreover, many educators say they see themselves as perpetual students, and they want to role-model and share with their students a sense of wonderment, a healthy skepticism, a passion for truth, and beauty and good, among other things. Does it make sense for educators to talk this way?

How would you distinguish educators from trainers? How would you distinguish education from training? If language were not a problem, do you think people from one culture could go to another culture and recognize the difference between students being educated and trainees being trained? How could this distinction be recognized?

What exactly is education?

Appendix A

Resources for Further Information
An Annotated List

A WEBSITE AT SAM HOUSTON STATE UNIVERSITY

We have established a website at Sam Houston State University (SHSU) to continue to assist you as your time and needs evolve.

The website will serve several purposes. First, you can expect a return from us in four business days while schools and universities are in session each year. Second, from time to time, we post a new script on the website that will be freely available to all users of the system. Third, if a school or district at which you work after you get certified/licensed decides it would like a workshop or even a year-long piloted program in their district, they can contact the website to request one or more of the authors to respond and manage the request in detail. If no particular author is desired, the website manager at SHSU will direct your request to the author(s) he or she thinks might be most apt in working with the project you have in mind. Finally, there are a number of programs around the world that study communities of inquiry, cognitive development in teacher education, morality, and pedagogical professionalism, as well as the strategic sciences for more exacting thinking. The website will maintain a clearinghouse of such programs to the extent that we know about them. The address of the website is http://thinkingbeyondthetest.weebly.com. For additional information, the phone number to contact Dr. Daphne Johnson at Sam Houston is (936) 294–3875.

BOOKS ON ENGAGING STUDENTS ON COMMUNITIES OF INQUIRY

A. *Argue with Me*, 2nd ed. (2016) by Deanna Kuhn, Laura Hemberger, and Valerie Khait is available from Routledge. This book is based on Deanna

Kuhn's highly regarded, decades-long research study of argumentation skills, and it is a handbook intended to aid the classroom teacher in developing his or her students' skills at argumentation and, subsequently, their writing skills.

B. *Critical Thinking across the Curriculum: A Brief Edition of Thought & Knowledge* (1997) by Diane F. Halpern is available at Taylor & Francis. This is an abridged version of *Critical Thinking across the Curriculum*. It is designed to help students enhance their thinking skills in every class and in academic area. This is an easy-to-read book with many practice exercises.

C. *Becoming a Critical Thinker*, 8th ed. (2014), written by Vincent Ruggiero is available at Cengage. This book gives students the opportunity to develop critical thinking skills in the classroom while stressing its application to real-life situations. It also breaks up critical thinking into a series of cumulative exercises that are in the book.

D. *Asking the Right Questions*, 11th ed. (2014), written by Neil Browne and Stuart Keeley is available at Pearson.

E. *Thinking beyond the Test: Strategies for Re-Introducing Higher-Level Thinking Skills* and *Focus on Thinking: Engaging Students in Higher-Order Thinking* by Wagner, Johnson, Fair, and Fasko are available from Rowman and Littlefield.

These books were written in the wake of initiatives such as No Child Left Behind and the use of high-stakes testing. Because of these initiatives, the emphasis in schools has been on drill and practice for the test. Genuine understanding and critical thinking have been increasingly shortchanged. As a result, students have fewer opportunities to advance their insight into cognitive and emotional challenges, even though both teachers and parents recognize the importance of developing deliberative and reflective thinking skills.

The books uniquely combine two things. First, they provide resources for classroom teachers in grades three to six and seven to twelve, respectively, that make it possible for them, at a moment's notice, to take advantage of a teachable moment by drawing students into productive intellectual discussions. Second, they give the reader an overview of the rationale and the research base for engaging students in educational activities that are truly intellectual and that are not limited to training for testing success.

In each of the books, there is also an invitation spelled out in step-by-step fashion, for the enterprising teacher to go beyond the contents of the scripts in the books by creating his or her own scripts. That teacher then calls upon his or her own experiences and expertise to draw students deeper into the Great Conversation of Humankind.

INSTITUTIONS THAT SUPPORT PROGRAMS TO INVOLVE STUDENTS IN THE GREAT CONVERSATION

A. The University of Hawai'i at Manoa Uehiro Academy for Philosophy and Education at http://p4chawaii.org. This program has been ongoing for a number of years, and you can find all sorts of resources from a link on their home page. One of the important things this program stresses is how structured discussions of serious questions in the school classroom contribute to cross-cultural understanding. Here is a portion of their operating philosophy: "Schools must move from being institutions that provide students with extrinsic meanings to institutions that provide students with the necessary circumstances and tools that will allow each to personally construct meaning in their own learning and lives."
B. The National Council for Excellence in Critical Thinking (NCECT), Tomales, California. The goal of the NCECT is to articulate, preserve, and foster intellectual standards in critical thinking research, scholarship, and instruction. The NCECT is a creation of the Foundation for Critical Thinking. The aim of the Foundation and Center for Critical Thinking is to improve education in colleges, universities, and primary through secondary schools. Their website is http://www.criticalthinking.org//.

RESOURCES FOR CRITICAL THINKING THEORY, PEDAGOGY, AND PRACTICE

A. There are a number of textbooks that convey an overall sense of what can be involved in the effort to teach critical thinking principles and practices. A couple of the standard texts are *Critical Thinking: Consider the Verdict* by Bruce Waller (6th edition, 2012) and *The Power of Critical Thinking* by Lewis Vaughn (5th edition, 2015). Two innovative books in this area are *Reason in the Balance* by Sharon Bailin and Mark Battersby (2nd edition, 2016) and *THINK Critically* by Peter Facione and Carol Gittens (2nd edition, 2013).
B. In addition to Daniel Kahneman's book *Thinking, Fast and Slow*, there are several books by psychologists that should be of interest to anyone concerned with critical thinking, such as *Mindware: Tools for Smart Thinking* by Richard Nisbett (2015), *What Intelligence Tests Miss: The Psychology of Rational Thought* by Keith Stanovich (2010), and the classic *How We Know What Isn't So* by Tom Gilovich. See also *Risk Savvy: How to Make Good Decisions* (2014) by Gerd Gigerenzer for a somewhat contrarian view.

C. There are several websites that offer a variety of "takes" on what critical thinking involves. One is Insight Assessment, which is a source for some of the most widely used tests to assess critical thinking skills and dispositions (http://www.insightassessment.com). Another website that features materials inspired by the work of Richard Paul is http://www.criticalthinking.org//. For a sample of this approach to critical thinking, a handy source is *Learning to Think Things Through: A Guide to Critical Thinking across the Curriculum* by Gerald Nosich (4th edition, 2011). Here is a website that is off the beaten track somewhat, but it offers an approach to critical thinking as involving dialogue as an essential component: http://www.cog-tech.com.

D. Journals

1. *Inquiry: Critical Thinking across the Disciplines*, Sam Houston State University, three issues (print and online versions)

    Inquiry: Critical Thinking across the Disciplines is a forum for the discussion of issues related to the theory, practice, and pedagogy of critical thinking across the disciplines, from precollege to university settings. The goal is to encourage an exchange of ideas about effective pedagogy in critical thinking instruction, about methods of assessing critical thinking skills and dispositions, about systematic errors in our thinking, about enhancing the quality of information on which we base decisions and inferences, about common fallacies in argumentation, and about all other topics that are relevant to critical thinking across the disciplines.

2. *Informal Logic*, University of Windsor, Canada, quarterly (online version)

    Informal Logic is a peer-reviewed journal publishing articles and reviews on topics related to reasoning and argumentation in theory and practice. It is deliberately multidisciplinary, welcoming theoretical and empirical research from any pertinent field, including, but not restricted to, philosophy, rhetoric, communication, linguistics, psychology, artificial intelligence, education, and law.

3. *Thinking & Reasoning*, Routledge, quarterly (print and online versions)

    Thinking & Reasoning is dedicated to the understanding of human thought processes, with particular emphasis on studies on reasoning, decision making, and problem solving. While the primary focus is on psychological studies of thinking, contributions are welcome from philosophers, artificial intelligence researchers, and other cognitive scientists whose work bears upon the central concerns of the journal. Topics published in the journal fall under the broad umbrella described earlier and include studies of deductive reasoning, inductive reasoning, judgments of probability and other quantities, conceptual thinking, the neuropsychology of reasoning, and the influence of language and culture on thought.

4. *Thinking Skills and Creativity*, Elsevier, quarterly (print and online versions)

    Thinking Skills and Creativity is a journal providing a peer-reviewed forum for communication and debate for the community of researchers interested in teaching for thinking and creativity. Papers may represent a variety of theoretical perspectives and methodological approaches and may relate to any age level in a diversity of settings: formal and informal, education and work-based.

5. *Argumentation*, Springer, quarterly (print and online versions)

    Argumentation is an international and interdisciplinary journal that gathers academic contributions from a wide range of scholarly backgrounds and approaches to reasoning, natural inference, and persuasion: communication, classical and modern rhetoric, linguistics, discourse analysis, pragmatics, psychology, philosophy, formal and informal logic, critical thinking, history, and law. Its scope includes a diversity of interests, from philosophical, theoretical, and analytical to empirical and practical topics. *Argumentation* publishes papers, book reviews, a yearly bibliography, and announcements of conferences and seminars.

Appendix B

What You Wanted to Know about Action Research but Were Afraid to Ask

Action research is research that you conduct in your work environment about a question and/or issue that you would like to investigate. An example might be, after reading some research on increases in academic performance when students are taught to use what are frequently called mind maps, concept maps, or networks, you decide to try this technique with your own students. Or, for another example, is there a specific problem with a disruptive student in your classroom? If so, you might read some research on handling disruptive students to give you ideas that might help the situation, and then you try the ideas.

Before you act, it would be wise for you to have at least four sources of information to support what you are trying to accomplish. These sources can come from journals, the Internet, and so on, and the point is to see whether or not there is a research consensus on the topic—if there is a consensus you may feel more confident going forward and if there is not a consensus you should be able to say something about why you took the direction you did.

Because you are studying a topic/issue with your own students to be used in your class(es), you do *not usually* have to go through your district's human subjects review board. However, even if it is something as simple as a survey done with your students, you should still send a written form home with any students under eighteen years of age, which explains the survey.

In general, an action research activity includes the following steps:

1. Identify the issue or define an area you wish to study (e.g., conduct a needs assessment).
2. Describe how you will implement what you want to accomplish (i.e., your method).

3. Decide what type of data you should collect (e.g., frequencies), how it should be collected (e.g., observations), and how often it should be collected (at least two weeks for a classroom project).
4. Then collect and analyze the data. (You do not have to conduct any statistical analysis, such as a correlation, of your data.) This is also a time for reflection (Acosta & Goltz, 2014).
5. Describe and determine how your findings can be utilized and applied—this is your action plan and this is why it is called "action research."
6. Convey and/or share your results and action plan objectively with others, such as your colleagues and/or your administrator(s) (A. P. Johnson, 2003, 2012).

So what is the ultimate goal of your action research? As Johnson (2003) stated, it is "to use your findings to make effective changes or choices" (p. 21). Thus, make sure you have clear goals that describe why and what you want to achieve with your action plan. "The final measure of your action research is the degree to which it clearly asks and answers your question, communicates your ideas, and serves to promote positive change" (Johnson, 2003). Remember that you can always *revise as required*!

In answer to the question "Why action research?" Richard Sagor (2000, Chap. 1) gives us these four goals:

1. Professionalize teaching.
2. Enhance the motivation and efficacy of a weary faculty.
3. Meet the needs of an increasingly diverse student body.
4. Achieve success with "standards-based" reforms.

Finally, action research is an excellent method to link theory, research, and practice.

Appendix C

A Note to Professors on Building Their Own Scripts

In describing how to build your own scripts, we risk trivializing your understanding of the process. The description will make building a script sound much easier than it in fact is.

One must begin with a strong and broadly based educational background. In addition, one must be very alert when collecting practical experience. A competent script builder should always be summing and revising his or her sense of the world in which we all live (Lynch, 2004, 2012).

In sympathy with this point, British philosopher and pioneer in logic and democratic theory John Stuart Mill once declared that it is better to be Socrates dissatisfied than a pig satisfied. Mill meant that thinking should aim for understanding and not hedonistic satisfaction. When building scripts, the task is to tantalize and challenge students to relentlessly seek better understanding and shared explanation. The task is not to say things one likes or wants to be true. The task is to pave the way toward independent and shared ventures in truth-seeking for each and every discussion participant.

At the beginning of every disciplinary study, there is a need for some ritualized sharing of signaling as Robin Wiley describes it in his book *Noise Matters* (2015). From learning the alphabet and how to count and do quadratic equations, there is a need to be told or shown how to do something until the student gets it right. When learning anything, there is a threshold at which novices have learned enough to engage further material reflectively. This threshold to more reflective exercise is about recognizing when students have the patience and skill to pursue a line of questioning relentlessly.

Scripts entice students to ask two questions over and again. The first question that permeates all scripting exercises is "How do you know?" The second question is "What do you or I mean by the term X?" Most scripts also require a willingness to "finish" a script with an open-ended question somewhat rehearsing where the script began.

Plato's advice to acquire knowledge and experience before more serious thinking is sound. Take your time, and always consider revising a script after you have field-tested it with a class. When you find something that works, you will want to write it out in context lest you lose the valuable twists and turns you have carefully sculpted when engaging students in more freelancing, less disciplined inquiry.

PICKING A TOPIC

Step one: Pick a topic that excites you. When you are excited about a topic, it tends to be infectious to others. So, step one: pick a topic that excites you. Your interest and intrigue are likely to be infectious among your students.

Caveat: Your topic, while exciting to you, must also fit into the subject matter that the students are studying. This does not mean that the topic must be rubric-fashioned to anticipate test items on a standardized test. Rather it simply advises judicious discernment when selecting a topic relevant to what students are studying and prepared to draw upon as a result of their previous learning.

FOCUS

Step two: Once you have a topic in mind, narrow your focus. The great twentieth-century philosopher Ludwig Wittgenstein thought that language can often obfuscate rather than clarify an issue people want to understand more clearly. Define your terms. Both Socrates and Plato often give the impression that deeper understanding can be fleshed out simply by agreeing on the real meaning of essential terms. To sharpen focus, it is often advantageous to single out one or two terms as central to the inquiry you have in mind. For example, if you want to explore the idea of reasonableness, you might start by focusing attention on the word "reason."

KICK OFF

Step three: Once you have focused on one or two terms, it is time to think about how to start a script. Usually, it is best to begin a script by asking a question about the meaning of one or the other key words you have in mind.

For example, if you are talking about reasonableness, you might begin by simply asking the open-ended question, "What is a reason?" This is the way people enter into real conversations with one another, is it not?

Each of the scripts in this book has a title. The title is there solely for the purpose of indexing, distinguishing the content of one script from another. Never start a scripted discussion by announcing to students the title of the script. When you begin by announcing a title, you immediately move the discussion away from a genuine conversation to merely that of another classroom exercise. In the world outside of classrooms, people do not begin conversations by announcing a title for a topic they want to discuss. In the world outside of the classroom, when a person wants to initiate a discussion, he or she usually starts by asking a question.

Step four: In many ordinary discussions, the leading question is too often long-winded and contains a hint of the answer the speaker wants to solicit. This is not how the leading question of a scripted discussion is to begin. In a scripted discussion, the leading question should be brief and open-ended. This gives wary participants a chance to get their feet wet before stepping into full-scale reflective analysis and discussion with one another.

FOLLOW UP

Step five: Following the first question, there are usually further questions prompting participants more deeply into disciplined conversation. These follow-up questions are intended to lure the students into an early consensus on how to think about the matter at hand. There may also be an early exposition of a noncontentious example. The point at this early stage is to draw the students into a false sense of security that "we've got this!"

Psychologist Leon Festinger (1957) showed that, when students commit to the truth of something and then find that truth is in peril, they are generally more eager to engage in discussion to relieve the cognitive dissonance they feel. In the vernacular, we may say simply that when participants in the impending discussion feel they "have a horse in the race," they pay more attention to every turn.

In step five, questions are designed to move forward from an open-ended challenge to clarification of a concept discussants too readily assumed was uncontroversial. The original, tentatively held consensus gives everyone a horse in the race. Once off the starting line, however, it becomes evident to participants that all horses in the race are not lined up in uniform fashion. Differences of opinion and irregularities of competing arguments are then set forward to engage the most serious thinking of all.

CRITICAL REVIEW

Step six: Create grounds for critical review. Most typically this can be accomplished by creating a scenario that seems, on the surface at least, to run counter to the previous consensus. For example, if students seemed generally agreed that a *reason* is something that causes action, the scenario offered might show how a reason may *cause* a change of belief in someone. Students should then question whether or not a change in belief *necessarily* leads to immediate change in subsequent action.

To illustrate this point, one could devise a story about a young man who has been told that his ancestry is mostly German, but, after he sends his DNA away to be tested, he discovers that his ancestry is actually, according to the DNA, mostly Scottish. This does not have to lead to any particular action on his part, but he has definitely changed one of his beliefs. Similarly, one can discover new evidence about historical events that changes one's beliefs but does not necessarily lead to any specific sort of action.

Notice that the idea that reason animates actions has not been discarded in this scenario. Some students may argue that *actions of the mind* are like other *actions in the physical world*. The challenge then is to prompt these students to give an account justifying that possibility by asking either "What do you mean by *action*?" or "How do you *know* they are alike?" This invites students to give *plausible reasons* for hanging on to their initial intuitions. Other students who abandoned their initial intuitions about differential sizes of infinite sets should similarly be asked to explain their reasons for their revised convictions regarding infinite sets. Subsequently, all students should be asked whether or not their convictions about such matters are likely to lead to any changes in their subsequent actions in the future.

Step seven: At this point students are fully engaged in critical review of a concept. What do reasons do? What are reasons for? How do we know when we come across a reason? What is the connection between reasons and conclusions? What is the role of reasons in directing actions? What is the role of reasons in "being reasonable"?

At this point the scripter is posing questions in a logical sequence that slows students from jumping to conclusions. Here the scripter with a logical sequence of questions following the counterexample scenario is revealing to participants what it means to reflectively turn a thought over in one's mind as educational philosophers John Dewey and Matthew Lipman so often encouraged. This is the heart of the script. It is here that the scripter's talent is most prominently exhibited. Students should feel that they are engaged in a discussion that matters. They are seeking right as opposed to wrong, truth as opposed to falsehood, meaningfulness as opposed to nonsense, and utility as opposed to mere fancy.

All too often discussions in classrooms degenerate into a "hide and seek" format or to a "whatever" format. In the "hide and seek" format, students quickly catch on that the only point to the discussion is to get to the answer the teacher had in mind all along. When students feel that this is what is going on, it turns the discussion into little more than a simple game like Twenty Questions. In the "Whatever" format, the teacher announces that in the discussion we are about to have, there are no right or wrong answers! Truly? If that is the case, then why have the discussion at all? Isn't this what wasting time is all about? For a discussion to matter, students must sense it can be purposeful (Sher, 2016).

For discussions to be purposeful, they must at least hold promise of leading participants some distance away from errant and misguided conclusions. Guaranteeing truth does not need to be part of the deal. But progress away from error must always hold some promise of progress.

If students believe that there is no right or wrong answer to their discussion, then they are likely either to trivialize the exercise in their mind or to see it as little more than a competition to win their way over classmates (Gardner, 2011). The value of discussion gets lost from the outset in the "no true or false/no right or wrong" or "whatever" announcement.

Most scripted discussions are intended to avoid identifying any position as T-R-U-T-H. On the other hand, it is very important for students to figure out that while they may not be able to identify grand cosmic truth in any sense, their shared investigation can lead them away from many errors.

Leading away from likely errors is what makes such discussion so pragmatically attractive (Wittgenstein, 1953). The idea that students can figure out a way to free themselves from at least some errors in thinking through shared discussion makes the value of critical review invaluable. When discussions are set from the outset to lead nowhere, the discussions are unproductive. At the very least, every scripted discussion should embody at least the hope for students that, as a result of the discussion, they might understand matters better and that where diversity of position continues to exist, the best reasons available for competing positions have been made evident.

THE LAST STEP IN THE PROCESS

Scripting the conclusion challenges scripter egos! Remember that as a scripter, you chose a topic that excited you. Yet as a scripter you are duty-bound, pedagogically speaking to stick to the script and not enter into the students' discussion to sell or even share your own ideas.

Throughout the heart of the script, the scripter has placed landmines (counterexamples and questions that challenge overgeneralizations) forcing participants to dig ever deeper to justify their emerging positions. The "wrong position" at least in the scripter's mind may be emerging as the apparent heir to truth in most participants' minds. The temptation to engage the students off script to "right" the apparent wrong is powerful, but the scripter needs to resist the temptation. What matters in the end is that *any position held* by a majority or, a minority, is held with substantial evidence or argument weighing in its favor.

Step eight: One of the best ways to finish a script is to ask a question about the concept central to the discussion all over once again. This may even be a repeat of the question with which the scripter started. In the example discussing reason, the first and last question may be simply: What do we mean by the term "reason"?

FURTHER CONSIDERATIONS

The major steps to creating a script have been described. However, as the saying goes, "The devil is in the details." To address the details, we now talk about appropriate language, length, relevant examples, paragraphing, and a tactic we call "sneaking in scholars' names."

Appropriate language: The first thing to keep in mind is that scripts are intended to lead conversation not to manage them. The difference between leading and managing a conversation is much the same as the difference between leading and managing in any human collective endeavor. *Leading* is a matter of getting folks to embrace their own decision-making capacities. It means getting participants to follow a discussion because it is engaging in ways that matter. In contrast, when *managing* a discussion, one employs manipulative strategies to ensure the discussion goes in just the direction the manager intends.

Managers feel responsible for getting everyone to a previously dictated destination. In contrast, leaders lead by keeping a general shared focus before the mind of all participants. Leading a discussion means making it appealing to follow generally a path that leads to a satisfactory conclusion(s). Think about it. When teachers use scripts, the purpose is to inspire and share, not manage and direct.

Language, as well as social role, has much to do with which ambience is present. When teachers use scripts, they cannot avoid the fact that they are teachers. But teachers can be leaders as much as managers.

A teacher can sit down with a group of students after school and just talk. During these sit-down talks, the teacher talks in his or her own voice without trying to talk down to the students in a language he or she thinks students might be able to get. Of course, the teacher doesn't use "highfalootin" language that will go over their heads. Neither she nor he calculates what she or he thinks the students are allegedly competent to understand. In addition, during such sit-down talks, the teacher listens and questions the students about what they might not understand. The point here is that the language used in a script should sound like a sit-down talk. The language should capture the scripter's natural way of speaking.

If the teacher uses a word the students are unfamiliar with, chances are they will naturally come to understand the new word in context. This has always been the most natural way children expand their vocabulary. If the student doesn't understand a word, then if the ambience is a trusting one, she or he will ask, "What does X mean?" When writing a script, the language should also have a bit of "folksiness" in it. By this we mean that people sharing in the discussion should get the feel that this is a genuine but casual search for some sort of shared understanding.

The bottom line is when building a script, use language reflective of how you speak naturally in conversation. Sentences should *sound right* and not *read right*. A script is not an essay. It is a script meant to sustain animation throughout a conversation. Don't be afraid to use colloquialism. For example, in discussing the difference between good reasons and bad reasons, you might ask: "President Obama once said, 'You can put lipstick on a pig but it is still a pig.' Does that mean that even good reasons can't make a bad idea anything other than a bad idea?"

Colorful examples and analogies invigorate sit-down discussions and can do so when properly employed in a script as well. When a script succeeds, it produces a moment of the Great Conversation.

Length: Scripts for younger elementary school students should always be kept short. No more than a page and a half at most. Even though you are not dictating information to be embraced by the student's long-term memory, the limited attention span of young adolescents will make even the most cleverly constructed script a tedious task when the discussion lasts beyond thirty minutes. Scripts that create fifteen- to twenty-minute discussions are likely to be most effective.

As students mature, they can sustain their interest in a discussion for a longer time. However, that doesn't mean that effective scripts for older students need to be longer. What it means is that as students mature, scripts of varying lengths can be effectively employed. Longer scripts for older students may contain more than one counterexample or even a description of a situation contrived to set up further discussion. Keep in mind, the purpose of the script isn't to import information into student minds. The purpose of the scripts is to learn more effective use of ideas the student is already somewhat familiar with.

Relevant examples: As noted immediately earlier, the purpose of the scripts is to prompt the student to use more effectively ideas he or she may already have in place. Examples in the script are not meant to teach participants in the discussion new textual material for assimilation.

First and foremost, examples are intended to inform the student of a new wrinkle to consider in regard to the matter at hand or most often to create productive cognitive dissonance following conclusions that seem somewhat consensual among participants up to that point. For the example to be effective, they must either call upon experiences likely to be well entrenched in most participants' previous personal experience, or they must be enticingly provocative to hold participant interest as gasps of "Really?!" slip quietly through their mind as the new bit of information or exotic scenario does the job of piquing participant imagination.

Paragraphing: The more mature the students, the more novel or extensive the presentation of new information or an extended scenario may be. The less mature students need information delivered with optimal brevity and immediate employment evident in the unfolding of a scenario or a series of questions. Less mature students also need to be primed with truncated scenarios that prompt discussion or flow into an inviting question in no more than sixty to ninety seconds.

Sneaking in names of scholars: Think of this as a tolerable luxury. Scenarios should adhere to a *principle of familiarity*. The principle of familiarity states simply that scripted discussions should begin well within participants' collective zone of proximal development. Scripts are for developing reasoning skills and are not to be employed for purposes of test preparation or any other kind of memorization exercise. What students are to retain from participation in scripted discussions is greater skill of reasoning.

Paying attention to the *principle of familiarity* does not preclude using some language that may not be generally familiar to all student participants. As noted earlier, if the unfamiliar language captures the manner in which the scripter would normally have a sit-down chat with students on the schoolhouse steps after school, the students will probably catch on to the term in context.

In addition, in the ambience of a sit-down chat, participants are likely to feel comfortable in asking for clarification of any word they do not understand. The principle of familiarity is a strongly intended heuristic when building a script. Sometimes the scripter may so love a certain author that he or she wants to build the author's name into a script. On occasion, that is perfectly all right. However, the scripter must not give into the temptation of ever testing students over the name of anyone mentioned in a script lest the script deteriorate into nothing other than an exercise in Piagetian assimilation.

For example, we may find ourselves drawn to want to share with the reader now that many writers have made allusion to the distinction between knowing how and knowing that. The first one to do so using those exact words was the legendary twentieth-century philosopher Gilbert Ryle (1949). That tidbit of information adds nothing to what we are discussing here or anywhere else in this book.

Sometimes attributions are done to give credit where credit is due—especially in scholarly journals—but on other times, it may turn out to be little more than a bit of hero worship on the part of the authors. That is just fine unless digression finds its way into something readers begin to fear they will be tested over.

Sometimes the scripter may include a scholar's name on the oft chance that students might remember it and, if they do, fine. If not, again, fine. So, for example, in building a script on morality, a scripter might write, "There was a Greek philosopher long ago who thought it is impossible to figure out all the right things to do in each and every case. This guy, named Aristotle, thought the best we can do is look at our intentions to figure out if we are acting virtuously. What do you think? Is figuring out our intentions important to figuring out whether what we are doing is good or bad, right or wrong, or even just okay?"

Notice, Aristotle's name is slipped in conversationally. Some participants may recognize it vaguely as an important name and remember it. Others may forget the name almost immediately and focus in on the idea of intentions or virtues. That too is just fine. If the student picks up a passing acquaintance with a great intellect, that might lead to some greater interest one day and that is fine. However, such learning is always incidental to the process scripts focus on. The incidental should never distract participants from learning from the core process.

Your script focuses on the process of thinking process rather than the outcome, but, if some participants incidentally remember that Aristotle was one of the architects of Western philosophy, that bit of "knowing that" is a bonus rather than an interference with the "learning how" to think critically focus of instruction.

There is one other reason for slipping in a name. A script developed for a particular subject may also be a way to introduce a figure central to some studies ahead without making it a centerpiece of some didactic instruction aimed at some standardized test ahead. So a history teacher may find using the name Aristotle beneficial in context, a science teacher might find Mendeleev worth mentioning, and so on.

THE SCRIPT YOU BUILD WILL BE YOUR OWN

There is an upside and a downside to this rather obvious fact. The upside is that in building a script, you are investing in a discussion you are already excited about and likely to share affection for when introducing the script to students. The downside is that it is very difficult not to sell your ideas, leveraging your authority as teacher or scripter to ensure the production of consensus you favor (Zagzebski, 2012). Your task is to draw on your experience, research, and other learning to lead participants into a discussion. You must muster the courage to trust your students that the path they variously finish is not interfered with by your desire for them to see the world strictly as you do.

When you ask students if they learned from their participation in the scripted discussion, you will learn three things if the script was successfully constructed. First, you will learn that the students believe they learned a great deal about their own thinking in the matter. Second, students will report that they learned the ideas involved were much more involved than they initially expected. Third, they will report that they learned important things from one another and not just from the scripter downloading information. When students report awareness of their learning these things, you will have confirmation that you brought the students into a moment of the Great Conversation of Humankind.

References

AACU. (2002). *Greater expectations: A new vision for learning as a nation goes to college*. Report of the Association of American Colleges and Universities, Washington, DC.

Acosta, S., & Goltz, H. H. (2014). Transforming practices: A primer on action research. *Health Promotion Practice, 15*, 465–470.

Adams, D. (1993). *Defining educational quality*. Improving Educational Quality Project, Publication No. 1, Biennial Report. Arlington, VA: Institute for International Research.

Aldeman, C. (2016). *Grading schools*. Retrieved from Bellwether Education Partners at http://bellwethereducation.org/

Almossawi, A. (2017). *Bad choices: How algorithms can help you think better and live happier*. New York, NY: Viking.

Anderson, L. W., Krathwohl, D. R., Airasian, P., Cruikshank, K., Mayer, R., Pintrich, P., et al. (Eds.). (2001). *A taxonomy for learning, teaching, and assessing: A revision of Bloom's taxonomy of education objectives*. New York, NY: Longman.

Arbesman, S. (2016). *Overcomplicated: Technology at the limits of compression*. New York, NY: Penguin.

Aristotle. (2009). *Politics*. Revised edition by R. F. Stalley (Ed.), with E. Barker (trans.). New York, NY: Oxford University Press.

Bai, H. (2009). Facilitating students' critical thinking in online discussion: An instructor's experience. *Journal of Interactive Online Learning, 8*(2), 156–164.

Baker, S. (2011). *Final jeopardy: The story of Watson, the computer that will transform our world*. New York, NY: Houghton Mifflin.

Bandura, A. (1976). *Social learning theory*. Englewood Cliffs, NJ: Prentice-Hall.

Barber, T. C. (2011). The online crit: The community of inquiry meets design education. *The Journal of Distance Education, 25*(1), 1–16.

Beers, K., & Probst, R., (2017). *Disruptive thinking: Why & how we read matters*. New York, NY: Scholastic Teaching Resources.

Bermudez, J. (2009) *Decision theory and rationality*. Oxford, England: Oxford University Press.

Bigelow, M. (2010). *Teachable moments*. Retrieved from NSTA Blog at http://nsta-communities.org/blog/2010/04/07/teachable-moments/

Binmore, K. (2007). *Game theory: A very short introduction*. New York, NY: Oxford University Press.

Bloom, B. S., Englehart, M. B., Furst, E. J., Hill, W. H., & Krathwohl, O. R. (1956). *Taxonomy of educational objectives: The classification of educational goals. Handbook I: Cognitive domain*. New York, NY: David McKay.

Boostrom, R. (2015). Standards, rigor, and rubrics: Prefabricated critical thinking. In M. Tenam-Zemach & J. E. Flynn (Eds.), *Rubric nation: Critical inquiries on the impact of rubrics in education* (pp. 85–99). Charlotte, NC: Information Age.

Bowles, S., & Gintis, H. (2013). *A cooperative species: Human reciprocity and its evolution*. Princeton, NJ: Princeton University Press.

Brighthouse, H., Ladd, H., Loeb, S., & Swift, A. (2017). *Educational goods: Values, evidence and decision-making*. Chicago, IL: University of Chicago Press.

Brockman, J. (Ed.). (2013). *Thinking: The new science of decision-making, problem-solving & prediction*. New York, NY: Harper Perennial.

Brookfield, S. (2003). Critical thinking in adulthood. In D. Fasko (Ed.), *Critical thinking and reasoning: Current theory, research and practice* (pp. 143–163). Cresskill, NJ: Hampton.

Buber, M. (1958). *I-thou*. New York, NY: Scribner.

Campbell-Whatley, G., Dunaway, D., & Hancock, D. (2016). *A school leader's guide to implementing the common core: Inclusive practices for all students*. New York, NY: Routledge.

Center for Public Education. (2013). *Understanding the common core standards*. Retrieved from the Center for Public Education at http://www.centerforpubliceducation.org/Main-Menu/Policies/Understanding-the-Common-Core/Understanding-the-Common-Core-Standards-PDF.pdf

Centers for Disease Control and Prevention. (2017). *Overweight and obesity*. Retrieved from https://www.cdc.gov/obesity/data/index.html

Chew, S. L. (2012). Challenging students' core beliefs and values. In R. E. Landrum & M. A. McCarthy (Eds.), *Teaching ethically: Challenges and opportunities* (pp. 113–123). Washington, DC: American Psychological Association.

Chickering, A. W., & Gamson, Z. F. (1987, March). Seven principles for good practice in undergraduate education. *AAHE Bulletin*, March 1987, 3–7.

Chomsky, N. (2016). *What kind of creatures are we?* New York, NY: Columbia University Press.

Chomsky, N., & Robichaud, A. (2014). Standardized testing as an assault on humanism and critical thinking in education. *Radical Pedagogy, 11*(1), 54–66.

Christian, B., & Griffiths, T., (2016). *Algorithms to live by: The computer science of human decisions*. New York, NY: Henry Holt.

Cleghorn, P. (2002). *Thinking through philosophy, Book 4*. Blackburn, UK: Educational Printing Services, Ltd.

Coburn, C. E., Hill, H. C., & Spillane, J. P. (2016). Alignment and accountability in policy and implementation: The common core state standards and implementation research. *Educational Researcher, 45*(4), 243–251.

Cook-Harvey, C., Darling-Hammond, L., Lam, L., Mercer, C., & Roc, M. (2016). *Equity and ESSA: Leveraging educational opportunity through the Every Student Succeeds Act.* Palo Alto, CA: Learning Policy Institute.

Copi, I., & Cohen, C. (2008). *Introduction to logic* (13th ed.). New York, NY: Prentice Hall.

Costikyan, G. (2013). *Uncertainty in games.* Cambridge, MA: MIT Press.

Cuban, L. (2016). Education researchers, AERA presidents, and reforming the practice of schooling, 1916–2016. *Educational Researcher, 45*(2), 134–141.

Cuypers, S., & Martin, C. (2013). *R. S. Peters.* New York, NY: Bloomsbury Academic.

Darling-Hammond, L. (2007). Evaluating "No Child Left Behind." *The Nation.* Retrieved from http://www.thenation.com/article/evaluating-no-child-left-behind

Darling-Hammond, L. (2017). *Developing and measuring higher order skills: Models for state performance assessment systems.* A Learning Policy Institute report for the Council of Chief State School Officers. Retrieved from https://www.learningpolicyinstitute.org/sites/default/files/product-files/Models_State_Performance_Assessment_Systems_REPORT.pdf

Deming, W. E. (2013). *The essential Deming: Leadership principles from the father of quality.* J. N. Orsini (Ed.). New York, NY: McGraw-Hill.

Dennett, D. (2017). *From bacteria to Bach and back: The evolution of minds.* New York, NY: Norton.

Deutsch, D. (2012). *The beginning of infinity: Explorations that transformed the world.* New York, NY: Penguin.

Dewey, J. (1916). *Democracy and education.* New York, NY: Macmillan.

Domingos, P. (2015). *The master algorithm: How the quest for the ultimate learning machine will remake our world.* New York, NY: Basic Books.

Dumitru, D. (2012). Communities of inquiry. A method to teach. *Procedia—Social and Behavioral Sciences, 33,* 238–242.

Dwyer, C. P. (2017). *Critical thinking: Conceptual perspectives and practical guidelines.* New York, NY: Cambridge University Press.

Edmonds, R. (1979). Effective schools for the urban poor. *Educational Leadership, 37,* 15–18, 20–24.

Ennis, R. (1969). *Ordinary logic.* New York, NY: Prentice-Hall.

Fair, F., Haas, L., Gardosik, C., Johnson, D., Price, D., & Leipnik, O. (2015a). Socrates in the schools from Scotland to Texas: Replicating a study on the effects of a philosophy for children program. *Journal of Philosophy in Schools, 2*(1), 18–37.

Fair, F., Haas, L., Gardosik, C., Johnson, D., Price, D., & Leipnik, O. (2015b). Socrates in the schools: Gains at three-year follow-up. *Journal of Philosophy in Schools, 2*(2), 5–16.

Feldman, R. S. (2017). *Life span development: A topical approach*. Boston, MA: Pearson.

Festinger, L. (1957). *A theory of cognitive dissonance*. Stanford, CA: Stanford University Press.

Gardner, H. (1990). Foreword. In V. Howard (Ed.), *Varieties of thinking* (pp. ii–ix). New York, NY: Routledge.

Gardner, H. (2011). *Truth, beauty and goodness reframed: Education for the virtues in the age of truthiness and Twitter*. New York, NY: Basic Books.

Garrison, D. R. (1991). Critical thinking and adult education: A conceptual model for developing critical thinking in adult learners. *International Journal of Lifelong Education, 10*, 287–303.

Garrison, D. R. (2016). *Thinking collaboratively: Learning in a community of inquiry*. New York, NY: Routledge.

Garrison, D. R., Anderson, T., & Archer, W. (2000). Critical inquiry in a text-based environment: Cognitive conferencing in higher education. *The Internet in Higher Education, 2*(2–3), 87–105.

Gerber, S., & Scott, L. (2011). Gamers and gaming context: Relationship to critical thinking. *British Journal of Educational Technology, 42*, 842–845.

Gigerenzer, G. (2002). *Calculated risk: How to know when numbers deceive you*. New York, NY: Simon & Schuster.

Gigerenzer, G. (2015). *Risk savvy: How to make good decisions*. New York, NY: Penguin.

Gigerenzer, G., & Todd, P. M. (1999). *Simple heuristics that make us smart*. Oxford, England: Oxford University Press.

Gill, B., Lerner, J., & Meosky, P. (2016). Reimagining accountability in K-12 education. *Behavioral Science and Policy, 2*(1), 57–70.

Gilovich, T., & Ross, L. (2015). *The wisest one in the room: How you can benefit from social psychology's most powerful insights*. New York, NY: Free Press.

Gintis, H. (2017). *Individuality and entanglement: The moral and material bases of social life*. Princeton, NJ: Princeton University Press.

Glass, G. (2016). One hundred years of research: Prudent aspirations. *Educational Researcher, 45*(2), 69–72.

Gormley, W. T. (2017). *The critical advantage: Developing critical thinking skills in school*. Cambridge, MA: Harvard University Press.

Gould, S. (2002). *The structure of evolutionary theory*. Cambridge, MA: Harvard University Press.

Graham, S. (2014). *Bullying: A module for teachers*. The American Psychological Association. Retrieved from http://www.apa.org/education/k12/bullying.aspx

Groen, M. (2012). NCLB—The educational accountability paradigm in historical perspective. *American Educational History Journal, 39*(1), 1–14.

Hacker, A. (2016). *The math myth: And other STEM delusions*. New York, NY: New Press.

Hacking, I. (2006). *The emergence of probability: A philosophical study of early ideas about probability* (2nd ed.) New York, NY: University of Cambridge Press.

Hain, A. B., & Piper, C. (2016). PARCC as a case study in understanding the design of large-scale assessment in the era of Common Core State Standards. In H. Jiao &

R. Lissitz (Eds.), *The next generation of testing: Common core standards, smarter-balanced, PARCC, and the national testing movement* (pp. 29–47). Charlotte, NC: Information Age.

Hancock, L. (2011). *Why are Finland's schools successful?* Retrieved from http://www.smithsonianmag.com/innovation/why-are-finlands-schools-successful-49859555/

Hand, D. (2014). *The improbability principle: Why coincidences, miracles and rare events happen every day.* New York, NY: Scientific American Press.

Helfland, D. J. (2016). *A survival guide to the misinformation age: Scientific habits of mind.* New York, NY: Columbia University Press.

Hirsch, E. (2016). *What your fourth grader needs to know (revised and updated): Fundamentals of good fourth-grade education.* New York, NY: Bantam (Penguin Random House imprint).

Hirst, P. (1975). *Knowledge and the curriculum.* New York: NY: Routledge.

Jackson, P. (2012). *What is education?* Chicago, IL: University of Chicago Press.

Jenkins, R. (2017, February). What is critical thinking, anyway? *The Chronicle of Higher Education: Vitae Community.* Retrieved from https://chroniclevitae.com/news/1691-what-is-critical-thinking-anyway

Johnson, A. P. (2003). *What every teacher should know about action research.* Boston, MA: Allyn & Bacon.

Johnson, A. P. (2012). *A short guide to action research* (4th ed.). Boston, MA: Pearson.

Johnson, J. H., & Gluck, M. (2016). *Every data: The misinformation hidden in the little data you consume every day.* Brookline, MA: Bibliomotion.

Johnson, S. K. (2012, December 14). Re-thinking the way colleges teach critical thinking [Blog post]. Retrieved from http://www.scientificamerican.com

Kahneman, D. (2013). *Thinking, fast and slow.* New York, NY: Farrar, Straus & Giroux.

Karp, S. (2013/2014). The problems with the common core. *Rethinking Schools, 28*(2). Retrieved from http://www.rethinkingschools.org/archive/28_02/28_02_karp.shtml

Kennedy, D., & Kennedy, N. S. (2013). Community of philosophical inquiry online and off: Retrospectus and prospectus. In Z. Akyol & D. R. Garrison (Eds.), *Educational commitments of inquiry: Theoretical framework, research and practice* (pp. 12–29). Hershey, PA: IGI Global.

Kerr, C. (1996). The ethics of knowledge. In L. Fisch (Ed.), *Ethical dimensions of college and university teaching: Understanding and honoring the special relationship between teachers and students* (pp. 55–56). San Francisco, CA: Jossey-Bass.

Kierstead, F., & Wagner, P. (1993). *The ethical, legal, and multicultural foundations of teaching.* New York, NY: McGraw-Hill.

King, J. E. (2016). We may well become accomplices: To rear a generation of spectators is not to educate at all. *Educational Researcher, 45*(2), 159–172.

Klarreich, E. (2017). In game theory, no clear path to equilibrium. *Quanta Magazine.* Retrieved from https://www.quantamagazine.org/in-game-theory-no-clear-path-to-equilibrium-20170718/

Koretz, D. (2008). *Measuring up: What educational testing really tells us.* Cambridge, MA: Harvard University Press.

Kuhn, D. (1999). A developmental model of critical thinking. *Educational Researcher, 28*(2), 16–26, 46.

Kuhn, D. (2015). Thinking together and alone. *Educational Researcher, 44*(1), 46–53.

Kvanvig, J. (2014). *Rationality and reflection.* Oxford, England: Oxford University Press.

Ladson-Billings, G. (2016). And then there is this thing called the curriculum: Organizations, imagination and mind. *Educational Researcher, 45*(2), 100–104.

Landsman, J., & Gorski, P. (2007). Countering standardization. *Educational Leadership, 64*(8), 40–44.

Langford, N. T. (2016). Decision theory applied to selecting the winners, ranking and classification. *Journal of Educational and Behavioral Statistics, 4,* 420–442.

Lerner, J., & Tetlock, P. (1999). Accounting for the effects of accountability. *Psychological Bulletin, 125,* 255–275.

Levitin, D. J. (2016). *Weaponized lies: How to think critically in the post-truth era.* New York, NY: Dutton.

Lickona, T. (1996). Eleven principles of effective character education. *Journal of Moral Education, 25,* 93–100.

Lindgren, H. C., & Suter, W. N. (1985). *Educational psychology in the classroom* (7th ed.). Monterey, CA: Brooks/Cole.

Lipman, M. (2003). *Thinking in education* (2nd ed.). New York, NY: Cambridge University Press.

Lynch, M. P. (2004). *True to life: Why truth matters.* Cambridge, MA: MIT Press.

Lynch, M. P. (2012). *In praise of reason.* Cambridge, MA: MIT Press.

Madsbjerg, C. (2017). *Sensemaking: The power of the humanities in the age of the algorithm.* New York, NY: Hachette Books.

Maestripieri, D. (2012). *Games primates play: An undercover investigation of the evolution and economics of human relationships.* New York, NY: Basic Books.

Maiorana, V. P. (2016). *Preparation for critical instruction: How to explain subject matter while teaching all learners to think, read and write critically.* Rowman & Littlefield.

Manley, R., & Hawkins, R. (2010). *Designing school systems for all students: A toolbox to fix America's schools.* Lanham, MD: Rowman & Littlefield.

Maslow, A. H. (1954). *Motivation and personality.* New York, NY: Harper & Row.

Maslow, A. H. (1970). *Motivation and personality* (2nd ed.). New York, NY: Harper & Row.

Mayo, E. (1933). *The human problems of an industrial civilization.* New York, NY: Routledge.

Mazur, J. (2016). *Fluke: The math of coincidence.* New York, NY. Basic Books.

McDonnell, L. M., & Weatherford, M. E. (2016). Recognizing the political in implementation research. *Educational Researcher, 45*(4), 233–242.

Mei, L. (2009). Bridging disciplinary boundaries. *Education Canada, 49*(3), 40–43.

Meichenbaum, D. (1985). Teaching thinking: A cognitive-behavioral perspective. In S. F. Chipman, J. W. Segal, & R. Glaser (Eds.), *Thinking and learning skills, vol. 2: Research and open questions* (pp. 407–426). Hillsdale, NJ: Erlbaum.

Meyer, S. (2013). *Darwin's doubt.* New York, NY: HarperCollins.

Miller, G. A. (1956). The magic number 7 plus or minus 2: The limits on our capacity for information processing. *Psychological Review, 63*, 81–97.

Ministry of Education, Singapore. (2016). *Education*. Retrieved from https://www.moe.gov.sg/education

Minnich, E. K. (2003). Teaching thinking: Moral and political considerations. *Change: The Magazine of Higher Learning, 35*(5), 18–24.

Misak, C. (2016). *Cambridge pragmatists: From Pierce and James to Ramsey and Wittgenstein*. Oxford, England: Oxford University Press.

Mlodinow, L. (2015). *The upright thinkers: The human journey from living in the trees to understanding the cosmos*. New York, NY: Pantheon.

Moore, B., & Stanley, T. (2010). *Critical thinking and formative assessments*. Florence, KY: Routledge (Taylor & Francis Group LLC).

Murray, H., Gillese, E., Lennon, M., Mercer, P., & Robinson, M. (1996). Ethical principles for college and university teaching. In L. Fisch (Ed.), *Ethical dimensions of college and university teaching: Understanding and honoring the special relationship between teachers and students* (pp. 57–63). San Francisco, CA: Jossey-Bass.

Newell, A., Shaw, J. C., & Simon, H. A. (1958). Elements of a theory of problem-solving. *Psychological Review, 65*, 151–166.

Nichols, S., Glass, G., & Berliner, D. (2012). High-stakes testing and student achievement: Updated analyses with NAEP data. *Education Policy Analysis Archives, 20*(20), 1–30.

Nowak, M. (2006). Five rules for the evolution of cooperation. *Science, 314*, 1560–1563.

Nowak, M., & Coakley, S. (Eds.). (2013). *Evolution, games, and God: The principles of cooperation*. Cambridge, MA: Harvard University Press.

Nowak, M., & Highfield, R. (2011). *Supercooperators: Evolution, altruism and human behavior: What we need from one another to succeed*. New York, NY: Simon & Schuster.

Nozick, R. (2001). *Invariances: The structure of the objective world*. Cambridge, MA: Harvard University Press.

O'Neil, C. (2016). *Weapons of math destruction: How big data increases inequality and threatens democracy*. New York, NY: Corwin.

Ortega y Gasset, J. (1985). *The revolt of the masses* (A. Kerrigan, trans.). New York, NY: University of Notre Dame Press in association with W. W. Norton.

Pais, A. (1982). *Subtle is the Lord: The science and the life of Albert Einstein*. New York, NY: Oxford University Press.

Pascal, B. (1671/1995). *The Pensées* (A. J. Krailsheimer, trans.). New York, NY: Penguin.

Paul, R. (1993). *Critical thinking: What every person needs to survive in a rapidly changing world* (3rd ed.). Tomales, CA: Foundation for Critical Thinking.

Perkins, D. N., Jay, E., & Tishman, S. (1993). New conception of thinking from ontology to education. *Educational Psychologist, 28*, 67–85.

Peters, R. S. (1966). *Ethics and education*. New York, NY: Scott Foresman.

Peterson, C., & Seligman, M. (2003). *Character strengths and virtues: A handbook and classification*. New York, NY: American Psychological Association in conjunction with Oxford University Press.

Peterson, M. (2017). *Introduction to decision theory*. Oxford, England: Oxford University Press.

Polikoff, M. (2014). *Common Core State Standards assessments: Challenges and opportunities*. Retrieved from the Center for American Progress at https://www.americanprogress.org/issues/education/reports/2014/04/17/88140/common-core-state-standards-assessments/

Polikoff, M., Porter, A., & Smithson, J. (2011). How well aligned are state assessment of student achievement with state content standards? *American Educational Research Journal, 48*, 965–995.

Poundstone, W. (1988). *The labyrinths of reason: Paradoxes, puzzles, and the frailty of knowledge*. New York, NY: Doubleday.

Qualters, D. M. (2017, January). Navigating ethical waters in the college classroom. *Faculty Focus*. Retrieved from Magna Publications at http://magnapubs.com

Raeburn, P., & Zollman, K. (2016). *The game theorist's guide to parenting: How the science of strategic thinking can help you deal with the toughest negotiators you know—your kids*. New York, NY: Scientific American Press.

Rescher, N. (1985). *Pascal's wager*. South Bend, IN: Notre Dame University Press.

Robertson, L. (2016). *Dueling claims on crime trend*. Retrieved from http://www.factcheck.org/2016/07/dueling-claims-on-crime-trend/

Ryle, G. (1949, reprint 2002). *The concept of mind* (1st ed.). Chicago, IL: University of Chicago Press.

Ryle, G. (1954). *Dilemmas*. New York, NY: Cambridge University Press.

Sagor, R. (2000). *Guiding school improvement with action research*. Alexandria, VA: ACSD Books. Chapter 1 is found at http://www.ascd.org/publications/books/100047/chapters/What-Is-Action-Research¢.aspx

Sapolsky, R. (2017). *Behave: The biology of humans at our best and worst*. New York, NY: Penguin.

Scheffler, I. (1990). *On human potential*. New York, NY: Routledge.

Schelling, T. (1960, reprint 1981). *The strategy of conflict*. Cambridge, MA: Harvard University Press.

Schelling, T. (1967, reprint 2008). *Arms and influence*. New Haven, CT: Yale University Press.

Schelling, T. (1978, revised 2006). *Micromotives and macrobehavior*. New York, NY: W. W. Norton.

Searle, J. (2001). *Rationality in action*. Cambridge, MA: MIT Press.

Secolsky, C., Judd, T, Magaram, E., Levy, S., Kossar, B., & Reese, G. (2016). Using think-aloud protocols to uncover misconceptions and improve developmental math instruction: An exploratory study. *Numeracy, 9*(1), Article 6.

Shannon, G. S., & Bylsma, P. (2007). *The nine characteristics of high-performing schools: A research-based resource for schools and districts to assist with improving student learning* (2nd ed.). Olympia, WA: OSPI.

Sher, G. (2016). *Epistemic friction: An essay on knowledge, truth and logic*. Oxford, England: Oxford University Press.

Shermis, M., & DiVesta, F. J. (2011). *Classroom assessment in action*. Lanham, MD. Rowman & Littlefield.

Siegel, H. (2017). *Education's epistemology: Rationality, diversity, and critical thinking.* New York, NY: Oxford University Press.

Simon, S. (2013). PISA results: "Educational stagnation." *POLITICO.* Retrieved from http://www.politico.com/story/2013/12/education-international-test-results-100575

Skyrms, B. (2014). *Social dynamics.* New York, NY: Oxford University Press.

Slavin, R. E. (2015). *Educational psychology: Theory and practice* (11th ed.). Boston, MA: Pearson.

Sloman, S., & Fernbach, P. (2017). *The knowledge illusion.* New York, NY: Riverhead Books.

Smith, G. (2014). *Standard deviations: Flawed assumptions, tortured data and other ways to lie with statistics.* New York, NY: Overlook Press.

Smith, G. (2016). *What the luck? The surprising role of chance in our everyday lives.* New York, NY: Overlook Press.

Smith, V. G., & Szymanski, A. (2013). Critical thinking: More than test scores. *NCPE: International Journal of Educational Leadership Preparation, 8*(2), 16–25.

Sober, E., & Wilson, D. S. (1998). *Unto others: The evolution and psychology of unselfish behavior.* Cambridge, MA: Harvard University Press.

Soni, J. & Goodman, R. (2017). *A mind at play: How Claude Shannon invented the information age.* New York, NY: Simon & Schuster.

Sterelny, K., Joyce, R. Calcott, B., & Fraser, B. (Eds.) (2013). *Cooperation and its evolution.* Cambridge, MA: MIT Press.

Sternberg, R. J. (2016). Testing: For better and worse. *Phi Delta Kappan, 98*(14), 66–71.

Sugar, G., & Tindal, G. (1993). *Effective school consultation: An interactive approach.* Belmont, CA: Wadsworth.

Sukel, K. (2016). *The art of risk: The new science of courage, caution, and chance.* Washington, DC: National Geographic.

Syed, M. (2016). *Black box thinking: Why most people never learn from their mistakes—but some do.* New York, NY: Penguin.

Taleb, N. (2014). *Antifragile.* New York, NY: Random House.

Texas Education Agency. (2016). *2015–2016 A–F ratings.* A report to the 85th Texas Legislature from the Texas Education Agency at http://tea.texas.gov/A-F/

Thaler, R. (2015). *Misbehaving: The making of behavioral economics.* New York, NY: Norton.

Thorp, E. (2017). *A man for all markets: From Las Vegas to Wall Street: How I beat the dealer and the market.* New York, NY: Random House.

Topping, K., & Trickey, S. (2007a). Collaborative philosophical enquiry for school children: Cognitive effects at 10–12 years. *British Journal of Educational Psychology, 77,* 271–288.

Topping, K., & Trickey, S. (2007b). Collaborative philosophical enquiry for schoolchildren: Cognitive gains at 2-year follow up. *British Journal of Educational Psychology, 77,* 787–796.

Tuomela, R. (2007). *The philosophy of sociality: The shared point of view.* New York, NY: Oxford University Press.

Tversky, A., & Kahneman, D. (1974). Judgement under uncertainty: Heuristics & biases. *Science, 185,* 1124–1131.

Valant, J. (2017). *As states submit ESSA plans, policymakers must design responsible school rating systems*. Retrieved from https://www.brookings.edu/blog/brown-center-chalkboard/2017/04/18/as-states-submit-essa-plans-policymakers-must-design-responsible-school-rating-systems/

Van Leeuwen, A., Poelhuis-Leth, D., & Bladh, M. (2016). *Davis' comprehensive handbook of laboratory diagnostic tests with nursing implications*. Philadelphia, PA: F. A. Davis.

Wagner, P. (1980). Are Plato and Ben Bloom et al. doing philosophy or "learning theory"? In D. Curtis (Ed.), *Proceedings of the southwest philosophy of education society* (Vol. 30, pp. 156–160). Fort Worth, TX: Southwest Philosophy of Education Society.

Wagner, P. (1986). Philosophical praxis. *Teaching Philosophy, 9*(4), 291–299.

Wagner, P. (1996). *Professional ethics: Fastback, 405*. Bloomington, IN: Phi Delta Kappa.

Wagner, P. (2006). Probability, decision theory, and a curricular approach to developing good thinking. *Journal of Thought, 41*(2), 23–38.

Wagner, P. (2010). Formalizing thinking for morally responsive administration. *Values in Ethics in Educational Administration, 8*(2), 1–8.

Wagner, P. (2011). Socio-sexual education: A practical study in formal thinking and teachable moments. *Sex Education, 11*(2), 193–211.

Wagner, P. (2013). Game theory as psychological investigation. In H. Hanappi (Ed.), *Game theory relaunched*. Retrieved from InTech Open Access at http://www.intechopen.com/books/game-theory-relaunched/game-theory-as-psychological-investigation, doi:10.5772/53932

Wagner, P. (2017). Warranted indoctrination in science education. In M. Matthews (Ed.), *History, philosophy, and science teaching* (pp. 307–315). Dordrecht, the Netherlands: Springer-Verlag.

Wagner, P., & Benavente-McEnery, L. (2008). The autistic society and its classrooms. *The Educational Forum, 72,* 319–328.

Wagner, P., Johnson, D., Fair, F., & Fasko, D. (2016). *Thinking beyond the test: Strategies for re-introducing higher-level thinking skills*. Lanham, MD: Rowman & Littlefield.

Wagner, P., Johnson, D., Fair, F., & Fasko, D. (2017). *Focus on thinking: Engaging students in higher order thinking*. Lanham, MD: Rowman & Littlefield.

Wagner, P., & Lopez, G. (2010). The great conversation and the ethics of inclusion. *Multicultural Perspectives, 12*(3), 167–172.

Wagner, P., & Simpson, D. (2009). *Ethical decision-making in school administration*. San Francisco, CA: Sage.

Weinrich, P. (2014). *Collective rationality*. Oxford, England: Oxford University Press.

Wiley, R. H. (2015). *Noise matters: The evolution of communication*. Cambridge, MA: Harvard University Press.

Williams, W. M. (1998). Are we raising smarter children today? School- and home-related influences on IQ. In U. Neisser (Ed.), *The rising curve: Long-term gains in IQ and related measures* (pp. 125–154). Washington, DC: American Psychological Association.

Willingham, D. T. (2007). Critical thinking: Why is it so hard to teach? *American Educator*, *2*(3), 8–18.

Wirt, J., Choy, S., Rooney, P., Provasnik, S., Sen, A., & Tobin, R. (2004). *The condition of education 2004*. (NCES 2004–077). U.S. Department of Education, National Center for Education Statistics, Washington, DC: U.S. Government Printing Office. Retrieved from https://nces.ed.gov/pubs2004/2004077.pdf

Wittgenstein, L. (1953). *Philosophical investigations* (G. E. M. Anscombe, trans.). New York, NY: Macmillan.

Wolf, N. (1991). *The beauty myth*. New York, NY: William Morrow & Co (an imprint of HarperCollins Publishers LLC).

Zagzebski, L. (2012). *Epistemic authority: A theory of trust, authority and autonomy of belief*. Oxford, England: Oxford University Press.

Zubrzycki, J. (2017, March 24). *Study finds common instruction materials in common-core states* [Blog post]. Retrieved from http://www. http://blogs.edweek.org/edweek/curriculum/2017/03/state_education_curriculum_common_core.html

Index

abductive thinking, 3–4
Abelard, Peter, 55
Academy Award winners, 81
accountability testing, 22
action research, 59, 123–24
Adams, John, 80
Aeschylus, 86
"after this therefore because of this" (*post hoc ergo propter hoc*), 67
AIDS, 83
Alexander the Great, 45
algorithm-driven technology, 1–3
Alice in Wonderland (Carroll), xii
Amazon Echo, 2
American life span, 82–83
analytical thinking, 59, 109–10
ancestry, knowledge of, 128
anorexia, 83
Apple Siri, 2
Aquinas, Thomas, 55
Arabic Moors, 83
argument, opinion compared to, 106
Aristotle: education purpose of, 49, 108; on expertise, 88, 91; on fairness, 42; laws respect for, 41; logic development of, 52, 55–56; name dropping of, 133; on self-actualization, 73; as teacher, 45

autonomy, 13, 15, 19, 37, 44, 73
Ayer, A. J., 98

Bandura, Albert, 13, 85
Bayes, Thomas, 57
Bayesian statistics, 8, 71
The Beauty Myth (Wolf), 83
behavioral economics, 66
Bernoulli family, 57. *See also* Pascal, Blaise; Bayes, Thomas
Big Blue, 8
big data, 48, 72
bike-riding, xiv
black box thinking, 3–4
Bloom, taxonomy of cognitive objects, 46
Boostrom, R., 21–22
Brookfield, S., 32
Buber, Martin, 6

Carroll, Lewis, xii
carrot or the stick, 7
CCSS. *See* Common Core State Standards
"The Charge of the Light Brigade" (Tennyson), 77
checks and balances, 78–84
chess, invention of, 113
Chew, S. L., 37

children fighting, 87
Chomsky, N., 19–20
classical economics, xi, 66
Cleghorn, P., 33
code-breaking, 98–99; computers and, 99
code creation, 98
code of ethics, 41–43
code instruction book, 98–99
cognitive science, xii, 65–66
COI. *See* community of inquiry
college enrollment, by gender, 83
Collins, Marva, 46
Common Core curriculum: argument against, 19; assessment of, 20–22; critical thinking and, 20–23; history of, 17–19; implementation of, 19–20; knowledge silos and, 23–24; reasons for, 19; standardized tests for, 17, 20–21, 23–24, 92; teachable moment and, 24–25
Common Core State Standards (CCSS), 17–22
community of inquiry (COI): critical thinking development of, 33, 37, 44; Great Conversation reinvigoration of, 34, 37; principles of teaching for, 33–34; respect in, 38; school classrooms as, 33–34; scripts use of, 33–34, 37
community of learning, 32–34; cognitive dissonance in, 32; deep thinking in, 32; metacognition in, 32; role modeling in, 32, 72
compliance, personal values and, 30–32
computational efficiency, education as, 5–7
conscientious reflection, 39
contemplative order, 76
conversation, hidden meaning of, 99
court packing, 79
creative thinking, xiii
The Critical Advantage (Gormley), xii–xiii
critical person, 109–10

critical thinking, xii–xiii, 20–24; closed-mindedness of, 52; gaming and, 68; information retrieval and, 4; role-modeling and, 53; scripts for, 37; values and, 29–44
critico-creative thinking, xii–xiii, 52–53; in community of inquiry, 44; for Great Conversations, xiii, 37; imagination and, 37; as innovative thinking, 33; for law of figuring things out, 51, 54; novel speculations of, 38; tools and strategies for, 55–73

Darling-Hammond, Linda, 18, 21, 26
Darwin, Charles, 60, 85
Dawkins, Richard, 81
decisions and choices, 84–85
decision theory: affairs of the heart and, 60, 85; for classroom discipline, 64–65; cognitive science compared to, 65–66; decision rule of, 62; decision tree of, *62, 64*; decision trees, construction of, 60–65; fast thinking for, 59; limits of, 65; for medical therapy, 63–64; for Saturday night plans, 61–63; tools for, 85
deep thinking: for Great Conversations, 9–10; guidelines for, 39; learning theory models for, 6; morality for, 7; scripting and, xii; strategies for, xiii; by students, 15; by teachers, 32, 49
deliberative reasoning, xi–xii
deliberative speech, 2
Deming, W. Edwards, 48
developmental courses, 18
Dewey, John, 49, 114, 128; Deweyan pragmatism, 12
dexterity of thinking, 4, 6
dialogical reasoning, 46–47, 51–53
divorce rate, 80
Dodgson, Charles. *See* Carroll, Lewis
dogmatist, and the truth-seeker, 102–3, 105

Index

Dresher, M., 69
drill and grill, 2, 9, 24

education: autonomy as goal of, 73; for better human beings, 1; change on verge of, 1–2; as computational efficiency, 5–7; as Deweyan pragmatism, 12; good, 1–15; as Great Conversation, 11; high tech economy and, 48–49; human betterment by, 29; ideal of, 7–10; instrumental value of, 108; Jackson on, xi, 12, 73, 114; medical, 2–3, 5; point of, 106–9; practice justification of, 108; propagandizing compared to, 107; as retrieval process, 2–4; rubrics for, 114–15; same, fair and equal of, 97–98; training compared to, 108, 114; vocational, 108
educator duties, 29
Einstein, Albert, 45
Eldridge, Niles, 81
Elementary and Secondary Education Act (ESEA), 17
empirical information, 40–41
entertainment industry, 79, 81
Escalante, Jaime, 45
ESEA. *See* Elementary and Secondary Education Act
ESSA. *See* Every Student Succeeds Act
The Ethical, Legal, and Multicultural Foundations of Teaching (Kierstead and Wagner), 39
ethical analysis, elements of: arguments pro and con, consideration of, 39–41; bear story for, 43; code of ethics for, 41, 43; empirical information attention to, 40–41; legal conventions review of, 41–43; logical operators use of, 40, 42; moral intuition use of, 40, 42; moral irresponsibility for, 43; moral nomenclature use of, 40, 42; self-interest avoidance of, 40–42; slow thinking for, 39

ethical and moral problems, 38–39
Every Student Succeeds Act (ESSA), 25–26
experiments, design of, 58
expertise, 88–91
exponential growth, 113–14

familiarity, principle of, 132
fast thinking: for decision making, 59, 64; as heuristics, 65–68; for law of figuring things out, 31, 66
Feldman, Gary, 5
Fermat's last theorem, 72
Festinger, Leon, 127
figuring things out, law of. *See* law of figuring things out
Fisher, Ronald, 57
flaw-noticing, 3
Flood, M., 69
Focus on Thinking (Wagner), 57
Franklin, Benjamin, 60, 85

Gallup, George, 80
Galton, Francis, 57
game theory, xiii, 7, 35–36; gaming compared to, 68; Great Conversation for, 68; prisoners dilemma of, 69, 69–70; slow thinking for, 71; STEM curricula and, 68; for Strategic Arms Limitation Treaty, 69–70; ultimatum game of, 70–71; zero-sum game of, 69
gaming, 68
Garrison, D. R., 33–34
generalization, sample based on, 57
gene sharing, 82
Gill, B., 26
girls, sports teams and, 81
Gopnik, A., 71
Gormley, William, xii–xiii
Gorski, P., 21
Gould, Stephen J., 52
government, purpose of, 107
Grand Rounds, 2
G-rated movies, 82

Great Conversations of Humankind: black box thinking for, 3–4; Buber on, 6; communities of inquiry and, 34, 37; critical thinking for, 35; critico-creative thinking for, xiii, 37; for Game Theory, 68; inductive reasoning for, 57; informal logic dispelled by, 56–57; for law of figuring things out, 72; questions of, 56–57; role-modeling for, 44, 47; scripts for, 49–50, 84, 108, 131; slow thinking for, 59, 66, 71; standardized tests and, 26; students in, 6–7, 29, 37, 44; teachable moments for, 15; teachers and, 12–13, 50–51, 72; thinking strategies for, 14, 46; Thorp on, 47

Hacker, Andrew, 48
Hampshire, Stuart, 98
Harris, Lou, 80
heuristics: availability, 66; imaginative, 91; secretary problem of, 67–68; to solve immediate problems, 66; thinking fast and slow and, 65–68; 37% algorithm of, 67–68
higher-order thinking, xiii
high-stakes testing: for Common Core, 17, 20–21, 24–25; critical thinking and, 23; cross-disciplinary focus and, 92; information retrieval for, 2, 9. *See also* accountability testing
Hirst, Paul, 49
homosexual behavior, 87
humans: emotions of, 10–11; generalized knowledge by, 91–92; genes of, 82; moral awareness by, 36; sensitivities of, 92
Hume, David, 10
hypotheses, testing of, 55–56

iconic geniuses, 45
IMPACT, 48
inductive thinking, 3, 59
infants, 10

inquiry, 34
intellectual dexterity, 4–6
intellectual progress, 1
interdisciplinary scaffolding, 23
Invariances (Nozick), 5

"Jabberwocky" (Carroll), xii
Jackson, Phillip, xi, 12, 73, 114
James, William, 45

Kahneman, Daniel, 59, 66–67
Kant, Immanuel, 73
Kelley formula, 5
Kierstead, F., 39
knowledge, truth compared to, 106
knowledge silos, 91–93; Common Core and, 23–24; integration of knowledge and, 23; questions answered by, 23
Kohlberg, Lawrence, 85–86, 101–2

Landsman, J., 21
law of figuring things out (LFTO), 50; for critico-creative thinking, 51, 54; fast thinking and, 31, 66; Great Conversation for, 72; slow thinking for, 60, 65–66; Thorp as master of, 47
laws, fallibility of, 39
learning program, 8–9. *See also* community of learning
learning strategies, 8
legal conventions review, 41–43
Lerner, J., 25–26
Levitin, Daniel, 52
LFTO. *See* law of figuring things out
Lipman, Matthew, 33, 128
logic, 52; fallacies of, 56–57; formal, 55–56; informal, 56–57
logical operators, 40, 42

Margulis, Lynn, 81
Maslow, A. H., 73
mathematical models, 48
The Math Myth (Hacker), 48

medical education, 2–3, 5
medical emergencies, 83
medicine, purpose of, 107
Medved, Deborah, 81–82
Medved, Michael, 81–82
Mendeleev, Dmitri, 133
Meosky, P., 26
Meyer, Stephen, 3
Mill, John Stuart, 45, 125
Miller, George, 3
Minnich, E. K., 22
The Minority Report, 82
Minsky, Marvin, 8
Mission Impossible, 82
Moore, Betsy, 22
moral: foundations, 35–37; intuition, 40, 42; irresponsibility, 43; relativism, 38–39. *See also* ethical and moral problems
morality, open-ended questions and, 110–11
morally sensitive humans, 8

National Center for Educations Statistics (NCES), 18
A Nation at Risk, 17
NCES. *See* National Center for Educations Statistics
NCLB. *See* No Child Left Behind
9/11, as teachable moment, 100
Nixon, Richard, 79
Nobel laureates, 81
No Child Left Behind (NCLB), 17–18
Noise Matters (Wiley), 125
Nozick, Robert, 5–6
nuclear reactors, safety of, 80

Oakeshott, Michael, 108
O'Neil, Cathy, 48
Ortega y Gasset, J., 49, 106
outcome based accountability, 26
over-fitting the data, 4

P4C. *See* Philosophy for Children
parallel processing strategies, 8

Pascal, Blaise: decision making father of, xii, 59; as genius, 45; probabilistic thinking and, 57; wager of, 60
Pearson, Karl, 57
pedagogical advice, xii
personal morality, compliance compared to, 31
Peters, R. S., 49, 108
Philosophy for Children (P4C), 53
physicians, purpose of, 106–7
Piaget, J., 71, 100, 132
Pierce, C. S., 3
Planned Parenthood Center, 30
Plato: cave of, 89; education higher end of, 108; essential terms meaning of, 126; on expertise, 88–91, 126; as teacher, 45–46
politically correct: as condemnation, 93; conflict avoidance of, 94; sarcasm use of, 94–95
Politics (Aristotle), 41
post hoc ergo propter hoc (after this therefore because of this), 67
pride, reason for: educational achievements, 95–96; GPA, 97; grade inflation, 97; textbooks dumbing down of, 96; understanding need for, 96
prisoners dilemma, 69, 69–70
prisoners of war, 83
probabilistic constructions, 57–59
product placement, 82
public opinion, 79, 84
Puerto Rico, emigration from, 81
Pythagoras, 55

randomized controlled clinical trial (RCT), 58–59
regression to the mean, 67
retrieval process, education as, 2–4
Rhee, Michelle, 48
Robichaud, A., 19–20
role-modeling, xi–xiii, 4; Bandura on, 13, 85; in community of learning, 32,

72; of critical thinking, 53; for Great Conversation, 44, 47; by teachers, 44, 71, 85–87
Roosevelt, Franklin Delano, 78–79
rubrics: for education, 114–15; teachable moments and, 101
Russian Jews, 83
Ryle, Gilbert, xiv, 132–33

satellite reconnaissance, 70
Savage, L. J., 98
Scheffler, Israel, 49
Schelling, Thomas, 70
school practices, 107–8
schools: as community of inquiry, 33–34; as community of learning, 33–34; evaluation of, 26
science, technology, engineering, and mathematics (STEM), 17; benefits of, 22, 24; big data and, 48; game theory and, 68
scripts, 12, 24, 26; building your own, 125–34; in communities of inquiry, 33–34, 37, 72; conclusion of, 129–30; critical review of, 128–29; educational background for, 125; examples for, 131–32; for Great Conversation, 49–50, 84, 108, 131; key words for, 126–27; language use of, 131; leading, and managing compared to, 130; position evidence for, 130; principle of familiarity for, 132; questions for, 125, 130; questions logical sequence of, 128; scholars names of, 132; standardized tests for, 126, 133; success of, 134; teachable moments and, 100–101; tips for using, 75–76; title of, 127; topic picking of, 126
secret codes, 98
self-actualization, 73
self-driving car, 6
self-interest, 40–42
Sessa, trickery of the maharaja, 113
Shannon, Claude, 47, 55

silos. *See* knowledge silos
slavery, 80, 89–90
Slavin, R. E., 73
slow thinking: for decision making, 59–60; for ethical analysis, 39; for game theory, 71; for Great Conversation, 59, 66, 71; for heuristics, 65–68; as intellectual strategy, 31; for law of figuring things out, 60, 65–66; as teachers strategy, 64
smartphones, 2–3
Socrates, 12–13, 45; essential terms, meaning of, 126; on expertise, 88, 91; as teacher, 98
software diagnosis, 3
sophists, 86
spymasters and codes, 98–100
standardized tests, xi–xii; for common core curriculum, 17, 20–21, 23–24, 92; Great Conversation and, 26; information retrieval and, 2; required by NCLB, 18; scripts and, 126, 133
Stanley, Todd, 22
stare decisis, 81
statistical evaluations, 57–59
statistical thinking, 59
statistics, 45–46
St. Benedict's Rule, 76
STEM. *See* science technology engineering mathematics
STEM curricula, game theory and, 68
students: autonomy of, 13, 15, 19, 37, 44, 73; cognitive dissonance of, 127; as deep thinkers, 15; dexterity of thinking by, 4, 6; drill and grill for, 2, 9, 24; Great Conversation and, 6, 29, 37, 44; intellectual adventure of, xiv; moral responsibility by, 7; motivation of, 14; patriotism of, 88; perpetual, 115; questioning attitude of, 109; role model learning from, 6; socialization of, 107; standardized testing of, xi–xii; teachers

judgment of, 58; vocabulary
expansion of, 131; wonderment
by, 11, 14, 115
Supreme Court judge, role of, 81
Syed, Matthew, 3
systematic thinking, xii

teachable moments, xi–xiii; finding of,
24–25; for Great Conversation, 15;
9/11 as, 100; scripts and, 100–101;
subordination of, 4; by teachers, 15
teachers: as calling, 44; checks and
balances and, 79; decorum of, 86;
deep-thinking, 49; differences in,
98; ethical responsibility of, 37–38;
evaluation of, 25, 48; as final
decision maker, 32; of good thinking,
12–13, 109–10; Great Conversation
and, 12–13, 50–51, 72; as leaders,
130; leaving the field, 24; literacy
test and, 96; as managers, 130; moral
commitment by, 29–30; as moral
educator, 85–88; moral foundations
of, 35–37; preparation scripts of,
75–115; professional commitment
of, 34–35; professional ethics of,
30, 35, 37; role modeling by, 44, 71,
85–87; as service professional, 109;
slow thinking by, 64; social attitudes
teaching by, 86–87; students
judgment by, 58; teachable moments
by, 15; values of, 101
teach good thinking, 13–15
technological innovations, 1
Tetlock, 25
Thaler, Richard, 66
thinking: abductive, 3–4; analytical,
59, 109–10; black box, 3–4;
critico-creative, 51–54; deep,
xii–xiii, 6–7, 9–10, 15, 32, 39, 49;
fast, 31, 59, 64–68; good, 13–15;
for Great Conversation, 14, 46;
inductive, 3, 59; morally good, 7;
slow, 31, 39, 59–60, 64–68, 71;
statistical, 59; wonderment of,
xi–xiii, 10–11, 13–14, 53, 72, 115
37% algorithm, of heuristics, 67–68
Thorp, Ed, 46–47
training, xi, 108, 114
travel, safety of, 83
truth-telling, 112–13
Turing, Alan, 98
Tversky, A., 67
twentieth century medicine, 82–83
Twenty Second Amendment, 79

unintended consequences: exponential
growth and, 113–14; law of, 61

vocational education, 108
Vygotsky, L., 71

Wagner, P., 39
Wainer, Howard, 113
Watson, 8–9
well disciplined, 76–78
What is Education? (Jackson), xi
Wiles, Andrew, 72
Wiley, Robin, 125
William of Ockham, 55
Wittgenstein, Ludwig, 126
Wolf, Naomi, 83
women doctors, 81
World Trade Center, 88

Zubrzycki, J., 20